The SmokeFree Formula
A Revolutionary Way to Stop Smoking Now

The SmokeFree Formula

A Revolutionary Way to Stop Smoking Now

Professor Robert West
with Chris Smyth
and Jamie West

*Are You Ready To Do What It Takes
To Stop Smoking?*

*This Book Will Help You Find
The Formula That Works For You*

This edition first published in Great Britain in 2013 by
Orion
an imprint of the Orion Publishing Group Ltd

Orion House, 5 Upper St Martin's Lane,
London WC2H 9EA

An Hachette UK Company

1 3 5 7 9 10 8 6 4 2

A CIP catalogue record for this book is available
from the British Library.

Trade Paperback ISBN: 978 1 409 14740 4

Printed in Great Britain by CPI Group (UK) Ltd,
Croydon, CR0 4YY

The Orion Publishing Group's policy is to use papers that are natural, renewable
and recyclable and made from wood grown in sustainable forests. The logging and
manufacturing processes are expected to conform to the environmental regulations of the
country of origin.

Every effort has been made to fulfil requirements with regard to reproducing
copyright material. The author and publisher will be glad to rectify any
omissions at the earliest opportunity.

The publisher is not responsible for websites (or
their content) that are not owned by the publisher.

www.orionbooks.co.uk

Contents

Thanks Go To ...   9

Introduction: Read This First   11

Part One: The Science of Stopping Smoking   **23**

Chapter 1: Understanding Why you Smoke and Find it Hard to Stop
                                                            25

Chapter 2: The Psychology of Behaviour – and How you Can
        Use it to Stop Smoking   45

Chapter 3: Addiction   63

Chapter 4: Why do you Want to Stop Smoking?   69

Chapter 5: Ways to Quit   77

Part Two: The Ingredients   **83**

Chapter 6: *Your* SmokeFree Formula   85

Chapter 7: Your Approach   95

   Ingredient 1: Stop abruptly   96

   Ingredient 2: Taking 'smoker' out of your identity   98

   Ingredient 3: Take it one day at a time   101

Chapter 8: Personal Advice and Support   103

   Ingredient 4: Professional stop-smoking advisor   104

   Ingredient 5: Telephone helpline   122

Chapter 9: Automated Support and Self-help Materials   124

   Ingredient 6: Text-messaging programme   124

   Ingredient 7: Stop-smoking website   126

   Ingredient 8: Another stop-smoking book   130

   Ingredient 9: Smartphone app   131

Chapter 10: Nicotine Products   133

   Ingredient 10: Licensed nicotine product   134

   Ingredient 11: Electronic cigarette   146

Chapter 11: Stop-smoking Medicines   154

   Ingredient 12: Varenicline (Champix)   156

   Ingredient 13: Bupropion (Zyban)   160

   Ingredient 14: Cytisine (Tabex)   161

Chapter 12: Staying Strong   166

   Ingredient 15: Plan things to keep busy   167

   Ingredient 16: Tell other people about stopping   167

   Ingredient 17: Count how much money is being saved   170

   Ingredient 18: Quit with friends or family   171

Chapter 13: Avoiding Temptation   178

    Ingredient 19: Change your daily routine   178

    Ingredient 20: Avoid smokers for a while   180

    Ingredient 21: Avoid alcohol for a while   186

    Ingredient 22: Go to bed early   187

    Ingredient 23: Get rid of all remaining cigarettes   187

Chapter 14: Dealing with Cravings   189

    Ingredient 24: Get active   190

    Ingredient 25: Isometric exercises   191

    Ingredient 26: Glucose tablets   193

    Ingredient 27: Mental exercises   196

    Ingredient 28: Breathing exercises   203

    Ingredient 29: Eat healthy snacks   206

Chapter 15: Your 'QuickStop' Guide: Creating your Own SmokeFree Formula   208

Chapter 16: Your Questions Answered   213

Chapter 17: If you Slip Up   227

Conclusion   239

Appendix 1: Things that I Don't Think Will Help   241

Appendix 2: The Benefits of Quitting Smoking   245

About the Authors   247

To my darling
Susan

Thanks Go To ...

I am deeply grateful to the tens of thousands of smokers and ex-smokers who have taken part in my research over the decades and especially those who have allowed me to use their stories in this book. Their generosity in sharing their experiences and doing what they can to help others to break free of their cigarette addiction is magnificent.

I also want to thank all those committed and highly professional stop-smoking advisors who are dedicated to saving the lives of others, and my mentor, and founding father of modern research into stopping smoking, Professor Michael Russell.

Grateful thanks go to Jon Elek, my agent, who had the idea and persuaded both me and my publisher, Orion, that it was a good one!

I am indebted to the stop-smoking advisors we interviewed: Jo Woodvine, Leila de Smidt, Andy McEwen and Ronnie Troughton.

I would like to express my heartfelt thanks to the smokers, stop-smoking advisors and communications professionals who so kindly commented on versions of the book: Andrew Faulkner, Aliyah Keshani, Anji Anderson, Cathy French, Dan Griffin, Emma Croghan, Heather Johnstone, Kate Knight, Karen Bromley and her daughter, Shira Litwack, and Matthew Alford.

Grateful thanks go to Cancer Research UK which funds a considerable part of my research, and to the English Department of

Health, Medical Research Council and several pharmaceutical companies that develop and manufacture smoking cessation treatments for their financial support over the years.

Finally, I am grateful beyond words to Professor Susan Michie who is my partner in every possible sense, who inspires and energises me in everything I do, and who is truly my better half.

Read This First

You're off to a great start! Whether you're standing in a book-shop or relaxing on the sofa at home, simply by opening this book you have taken a huge stride towards giving up smoking forever.

The SmokeFree Formula is a stop-smoking guide with a difference: it tells the truth, and it will help you make the truth work for you.

If you've ever searched the Internet, you'll know there's a huge amount of information out there about how to stop smoking. Unfortunately, much of it is wrong. If you tried to follow all the advice, you'd be trying to do several entirely contradictory things at once. That's because most of the advice out there is based on little more than one person's opinion or failure to understand the research evidence. You need a reliable source, based, not on guesses, wild claims or wishful thinking, but on the best research by leading scientists. That is what this book is.

Everything you will read here is based on the best available scientific evidence. I have devoted my 30-year career to discovering what works when it comes to giving up smoking. I head up a team of researchers mainly funded by governments and charities with one aim in mind: finding better ways of helping smokers who want to stop. This book combines my own research with findings from other leading scientists to give you the most accurate and reliable information there is.

So this book comes with a pledge: when I claim something is a fact, it will be backed up by hard evidence. I'll show you how to look directly at that evidence, if you want to. But there is still much that science cannot yet tell us. So, quite often I will give you my opinion. When I give you my opinion, I'll tell you it's just that. I will not dress it up as fact.

I want this book to be the best investment you ever make. I want you to be healthier, happier and have more money to spend on things that you can enjoy. I want to join you in your journey to a better life and be there to help you along the way. I can't do it in person, but I can do the next best thing through *The Smoke-Free Formula*. I will be with you for as long as it takes – and however many attempts it takes – until you are free from smoking for good.

The secret to stopping smoking

Here is the truth: there is no single miracle cure, no magic bullet, no one guaranteed method of stopping smoking that works for everyone every time. But there is a secret, and sometimes the best-kept secrets are out there in plain view. The secret is this:

Keep trying and each time do things that give you the best chance of lasting success.

Do this and you will find the formula that works for you. With your commitment and my expert advice you will find your own personalised SmokeFree Formula, which will help you be rid of cigarettes forever.

The first part of the secret: keep trying

If you follow my advice, there's a good chance that your next attempt at quitting could be the last time you ever have to try. But we both know there is a chance that you might have to do it again. In fact most smokers try quitting many times before they finally kick the habit for good. There are so many things that can go wrong and drive or trick you back to smoking: an argument with your partner, incessant cravings, feeling down, one too many drinks, being with other smokers, a moment of weakness …

There's no need to be discouraged by the thought that you might have to stop more than once. If you have relapsed before, you're in good company. I know how hard quitting can be, but I also know that so many people just like you have persevered and are now no more likely to smoke again than I am.

If you take only one thing from this book it should be this: you have to keep playing the game long enough for the odds to start working in your favour. You may become a non-smoker after one go, 10 goes or 20 goes. On the nineteenth attempt you may think you'll never succeed, and then on the twentieth – bingo! So *never give up giving up.*

In fact there's no real downside to having a go at giving up cigarettes. The worst that can happen is that you save some money, get yourself a bit healthier and learn something that will help you last even longer next time. The best that can happen is that you will change your life forever, live longer and become a happier, healthier person.

So please don't go into a quit attempt thinking that you will have 'failed' if you don't manage to stay off for good. That is such a common misconception, and it is so wrong. I really want you to think about it in a different way. You should feel good about every cigarette that you don't smoke: and if you keep at it, you'll break free from the hold that cigarettes have over you … permanently.

In this sense, you can think of stopping smoking as like looking for love: if you only ever went on one date, you wouldn't expect to have met your soulmate. Some people do, of course, and good luck to them. But if the first person you met wasn't right for you, you wouldn't give up, would you? You'd look for someone else. Because you never know when the right person might come along.

Trying to quit is like that: the right moment could be just around the corner. Every time you try, you increase your chances of stopping for good. I can't promise you love, but the rewards of quitting – a happier, healthier life – are also pretty good!

The second part of the secret: make every quit attempt count

If you leave everything to chance and just try to stop without using what literally billions of pounds and dollars of research has taught us, you may make it the first time or it could take a while. If you make use of the decades of scientific research compiled in this book, however, the evidence tells us you can expect to get there around four times faster.

Loading the dice

If you have played Monopoly or any other game involving rolling dice, you will have an understanding of the process of stopping smoking. Every time you try to stop it's another roll of the dice.

With dice, your odds of success – let's say in trying to get a 'double' – are no worse each time than they were before. And if you keep rolling, then sooner or later you are likely to get that double. That is what the research tells us about stopping smoking. It doesn't matter how many times you have tried in the past, the odds of lasting success each time don't go down, and the more you keep trying, the greater your chance of making it permanent.

But ... with stopping smoking, you can actually load the dice in your favour. You can improve the odds to help you achieve lasting success sooner rather than later. Put the right weights on the bottom of the dice and that double will come up a lot faster. That is what this book will help you to do.

With the right knowledge you can make your own luck. So the second part of the secret to quitting is to use your own experience along with the science in *The SmokeFree Formula* to give yourself the best possible chance every time you try to quit.

How the SmokeFree Formula works

There is no one way of quitting that works for everyone. This book will give you the facts you need so that you can decide for yourself what are the best methods to try on each attempt.

Over the course of this book, I am going to tell you about all the ways we know that can help you stop smoking. Everything that can help you quit is what I call an 'ingredient'. The ingredients do many different things and I will advise you on how to combine them in a personalised combination that will work for you. *This is your Smoke-Free Formula.*

What ingredients you choose to use is entirely up to you. My aim in this book is to give you all the information you need to help you to pick the best options for you. My motto is: *I guide – you decide.*

What will happen is this: Part One of the book will tell you why you *really* smoke – which is not the same as why you may think you smoke – and how you can tap into your reserves of motivation to get your quit attempt off to a flying start.

Then in Part Two I'll tell you about all the things you can use to boost your chances of success – from nicotine products, prescription medicines and talking to a 'stop-smoking advisor' to websites, physical exercise, deep breathing and many more. I'll then show you how you blend these ingredients together into your own personal formula to be free of smoking forever.

It's worth reading up on all the ingredients you might want to use because just as important as picking the right ones is making sure you use them properly. Here's an example.

Let's say you have stopped smoking and you are using a nicotine product such as the gum or lozenge to help you. Now let's say that you find that you are beginning to feel edgy and bad-tempered. Your friends are telling you to go back to smoking because you are becoming unbearable to live with.

You don't have to be. Being bad-tempered is a classic symptom of nicotine withdrawal and should be completely eliminated if you are getting enough nicotine from your nicotine product. Yes, you read that right – one of the most notorious and frustrating side effects of giving up smoking is completely unnecessary and will go away if you use your nicotine products properly. And most people don't. There are all kinds of perfectly understandable reasons why people fail to use enough of their nicotine products, but they are based on misconceptions that I can dispel. That's just one example of why expert help can be so useful.

Obviously I can't give up smoking for you – if I could, believe me, I would! Your mental approach is crucial. Just 'trying not to smoke' will not cut it. You need to make a commitment to quitting that involves a clear mental rule with definite boundaries. Normally this is quite simply: 'I will not smoke another cigarette – ever'. But if that is too daunting, it could be – 'I will not smoke for the next four weeks and see how it goes after that'. The crucial thing is that you set clear boundaries that you will not cross.

To stick to that rule you must make it part of yourself. You need to think about your self-identity as someone who may have smoked in the past, *but will not smoke in the future*. From now on, not smoking is part of who you are.

I'm not saying that you have to make the break immediately once you decide to stop. There may be things you have to do to prepare the ground – for example, you might decide to book an appointment with a professional stop-smoking advisor.

Once you are ready to go, I strongly recommend that you decide on a date within the next two weeks before you go off the idea. The research is pretty clear on this – if you set your quit date further ahead than a couple of weeks, you are much less likely to quit when the time comes.

If you are not quite ready, that is fine. As you go through this book you will learn more about what ingredients to put into your formula and at some point you will decide to take the step. Whatever your choice, once you have stopped, you have to be clear: right now, today, you will not take a single puff on a cigarette.

Are you ready to make that commitment? Here's a question to help you tell:

If you could swallow a pill right now that would make you never want to smoke again as long as you live, would you take it?

If the answer is yes, I think you are ready to quit. When you reach that point, you will benefit from help to make the most of your commitment, and that's what I'm going to give you. Think of using *The SmokeFree Formula* in three simple steps:

- **Go through all the shelves and pick your ingredients**

- **Decide on your personal 'quit smoking rule'**
- **Make sure you are ready for the big day**

- **Apply the rule and do whatever it takes to stick to it using the ingredients**

My story

I was once where you are now. I used to be a smoker and so I know from both personal and professional experience that quitting can be hard – but you can get there. My story is fairly typical in some ways. What is interesting about it is not so much what happened but how things might have been so very different.

Before I started smoking I was, like most children, very anti-cigarettes. My mother was a nurse and would tell me about the tragic cases she used to see of people with throat cancer or lung cancer – and smoking just seemed totally mad.

Everyone at school knew who the smokers were. You could smell it when, after break or lunch, they would come into the classroom reeking of smoke. It's funny when I think of it because it was against school rules and the smokers thought that the teachers didn't know, but of course they did – they didn't need to catch the children in the act of smoking, they just had to smell them in the classroom!

Anyway, when I was about 16 something happened. The people I liked were mostly smokers. I would go out to the local woods at breaktime and just hang around with them and chat while they smoked. Then I started borrowing cigarettes. It was only a social thing at first. I never bought them and so I didn't really think of myself as a smoker. Then, for no obvious reason that I can remember, I started to buy them. Perhaps my friends got fed up with me cadging off them.

The brand I mostly bought was John Player Special. They had a sleek black packet with a very stylish logo in gold. I thought they looked pretty cool. They weren't too strong – not like French cigarettes – and they tasted better than the most popular brand with my friends, which was Players No. 6 (very cheap – but very nasty!).

I never thought of myself as addicted but within a month or two I was smoking about five cigarettes per day. I could go for a few weeks at a time without a cigarette when I was staying with my father in Spain, but when I returned I would take up smoking again.

There were times when I really felt the need to smoke. I remember once I didn't have any cigarettes or enough money to buy some; I was on a station platform so I hunted down some stubs on the ground, teased out the tobacco and used an old bus ticket that I found in my pocket to roll up a cigarette and smoke it. It wasn't the most pleasant experience of my life, but it met a need.

When I went to university, my smoking increased. I used to act in plays, and that meant a lot of time doing nothing while waiting to come on stage – so I smoked. I was not the most studious of students and spent a lot of time in the Students' Union bar, where I honed my table football and bar billiards skills – and, again, I smoked. In my first year at university I probably got to about 20 cigarettes per day.

Early on, I don't think I ever tried seriously to stop smoking. I may have made some half-hearted attempts. I did notice, however, that it seemed to be affecting my health. Whenever I got a cold, it went straight to my chest and I would have a cough that seemed to last a long time.

In my second year at university I started going out with someone who didn't smoke and in fact hated the smell of it. When I look back at those years I realise that I was quite self-centred. It had honestly never occurred to me that my smoking was unpleasant for people around me.

Eventually, one evening I came back from a long rehearsal of a play and I had been smoking non-stop throughout – on stage and off. Finally my girlfriend cracked and made it clear – even to someone as thick-skinned as me at the time – that she really hated it.

I resolved to stop. It would not be hard, I thought. Except that it was. It wasn't that I got terrible withdrawal symptoms. It was not even that I needed to smoke all the time. It was just that whenever I was in those situations where I would normally smoke, I felt strong pangs of nicotine hunger. They were combined with a sneaky feeling that it would surely be okay just to have one or two – my girlfriend wouldn't know (yeah, right!).

So I went on like this for a few weeks at least – I was, so I thought, a secret smoker. It was like being back at school again. It is to my girlfriend's eternal credit that she didn't go on about it, though she must have known that I was still smoking.

The final straw was that it was actually harder to keep up the pretence of not smoking than actually to stop altogether. I think perhaps I must have cut down the amount I smoked quite a bit anyway, and I had one of those mind-shift moments where I thought, 'This is ridiculous – I might as well just stop'. So I did.

What lessons do I want to hand down to you from this experience? First, and most importantly, it may be pure luck that I did not end up smoking for decades and ruining my health. If I had gone out with a smoker in my second year at university, I almost certainly would not have stopped. If you are lucky enough to live with a non-smoker, treasure him or her – that person could be your lifesaver.

Secondly, my own experience very nicely illustrates what research into smoking has now shown us to be generally true – addiction to nicotine does not require you to smoke all the time. You can even go for weeks without smoking because you are in a completely different situation, and then feel the need to go back to smoking when you find yourself back in your usual smoking environment.

Thirdly, you may not be able to force yourself to have that mind-shifting moment when you think: 'To hell with this' – it comes from somewhere deep inside you. But you can set up the conditions that will make it happen of its own accord.

Smoking was a short interlude in my life. I liked the people who smoked who were my age. Most of us thought that we would smoke for a short while and then stop before it could do us any harm. A lot of people think that way, but – alas – it usually doesn't work out like that.

There is one final thing I want to tell you here, and that is the importance of *the story you are going to tell yourself* about how you quit smoking. When the going gets tough, are you the kind of person who will be able to say later: 'It was really difficult, but I battled through.' Or is it going to be: 'It was really difficult. I didn't make it on my first attempt, but then something happened and it was easy the next time I tried'?

In my opinion, everyone needs a story for their quit attempt. A narrative that helps you to make sense of what you're going through. Now is a good time to think about what will be your story. In five years' time, when someone asks you if you smoke and you reply, 'I used to, but I don't anymore,' how will you look back on your experience?

The prize

I'm not going to go on about how smoking is bad for you. You know that, or you wouldn't be reading this book. Instead, to start you on your journey, I'm going to give you some facts you might not know about the benefits of stopping.

They are important because at some point while you're reading this book, you will stop smoking. It might be for a couple of days, a week, a month or for the rest of your life. As you set off, hold this thought in your mind: *every time you try to quit is a success*. I will keep coming back to this because I want you to banish the thought that if you try to stop but go back to smoking, you have somehow failed.

Here are some of the ways you have succeeded with every day you do not smoke:

The first day

- As soon as you stop smoking, you cut your risk of a heart attack. That's because, when you breathe in smoke, your blood becomes more likely to clot, as your body struggles desperately to get rid of the tiny smoke particles that have got into your lungs. (It's the same process that leads to an increase in heart attacks in cities when pollution levels are high.) As soon as you stop inhaling smoke, this danger disappears.
- Within a few hours of stopping, the poisonous gas carbon monoxide – which you inhale in cigarette smoke and has been hardening your arteries – will vanish from your blood. And your heartbeat, which has been going too fast while you were smoking, will return to normal.
- Your hands won't shake as much. You might not have noticed it – or perhaps you have – but as a smoker you have a constant tremor. That's because nicotine overexcites the 'fight or flight' part of your nervous system – the same part that makes you shake with fear. As the nicotine leaves your body, your nervous system calms down.
- At the same time, the normal supply of blood will return to your hands and feet. You might have found that they often feel cold: that's because nicotine causes the tiny blood vessels in your extremities to close up. But a few hours after you stub out, that nicotine melts away and your hands and feet warm up by about 1° Celsius (1.8° Fahrenheit).
- If you make it just one day without lighting up, you've probably already saved more than half the price of this book.
- More than that: you could already have helped yourself to live six

hours longer. And six more tomorrow, and the same the day after; on average, you can expect to extend your life by six hours for every single day you are an ex-smoker. Quitting really is that good!

The first week

- Within a few days without cigarettes, your lungs will start to heal. The inflammation caused by toxins in the smoke will gradually subside and the tiny hairs that clear the mucous and dirt out of your lungs will start to spring back to life.
- You will smell better – in more ways than one! As your sense of taste and smell begin to improve, you will rediscover the true richness and flavour of what you eat.
- After just one week of not smoking, you can expect to gain, on average, almost two extra days of healthy life …
- … and save about three times the cost of buying this book.

The first month

- After a few weeks without smoking, your skin will start to improve. The wrinkles that mark you out as a smoker will start to fade away. The grey pallor will go, as colour flows back to your face. Stopping smoking is the best anti-ageing treatment you can get!
- You'll start to feel less stressed. Do you find that hard to believe? Many people think smoking helps them fight stress, and worry about how they will cope without cigarettes as a crutch. The truth is that, after a few weeks of not smoking, stress levels usually go down, so you can expect to feel more relaxed than when you were smoking.
- You'll feel fitter too. As your lungs recover you won't be out of breath so much.
- You'll save about 15 times the cost of buying this book – three times as much as the average monthly mobile phone bill.
- You can expect, on average, a full extra week of healthy life.

The first year

- After a year without smoking, your excess risk of having a heart attack will be halved.

- Your risk of cancer will have fallen substantially compared with what it would be if you had carried on smoking.
- You will have saved over 160 times the cost of buying this book, the same as the price of a really good holiday.
- You can expect to gain three months of healthy life.
- When you get to six months without smoking, the chances are better than evens that you will never light up another cigarette ever again.

The rest of your life

- As your life goes on, so do the benefits of not smoking. You'll *feel* healthier because you'll *be* healthier – being much more likely to avoid a huge range of problems, from dementia to diabetes, from hearing loss to heart attack, from chronic lung disease to cancer.
- You can expect to live up to ten years longer than if you'd carried on smoking.
- What's more, the evidence now shows that as an ex-smoker, you will feel happier and more satisfied with life.

Sounds good? Let's find out more about how you are going to get there ...

Part One

The Science of Stopping Smoking

Chapter 1

Understanding Why you Smoke and Find it Hard to Stop

It can be hard to stop smoking, no matter who you are. Here is a headline from 2011:

Barack Obama quits smoking after 30 years

Barack Obama has quit his 30-year cigarette habit after numerous failed attempts because he wants to be able to tell daughters he does not smoke, according to his wife Michelle.

The *Daily Telegraph*, 9 February 2011

Whatever your politics, I think you'll agree that President Obama is not weak-willed. Yet this man struggled to stop smoking for years, trying many times without success. In 2011 he was reported as having succeeded, and as far as I know he is still not smoking. If the president of the United States can struggle to stop, then anyone can – smoking is not a sign of weakness.

This part of the book explains the science behind smoking and why you have been finding it hard to stop. This will help because:

- It will reassure you that the difficulty you have had in stopping up until now is not your fault; the way I like to put it is: 'It's not you – it's your brain!'

- Once you know your enemy and the tricks it can play, you are better prepared to defend yourself against it.
- You will understand how some of the ingredients work, which might encourage you to try ones you weren't interested in before.

Science has told us a lot about why you smoke. I hope you find it interesting, but more than that: I think it will help you understand what you have to do to stay off cigarettes and why some of the ingredients listed in *The SmokeFree Formula* are helpful.

Reasons for smoking

Let's start with a questionnaire that has been filled in by thousands of people as part of my programme of research. You just have to look at the list and select the reason(s) why you smoke. Once you have filled it in, I will go through all the possible answers and tell you what other smokers said.

Reasons for smoking questionnaire
Which, if any, of the following describe how you feel about smoking?
(Put a tick by any that apply to you)

I enjoy it	☐
It helps me cope with stress	☐
I am addicted to cigarettes	☐
It gives me something to do	☐
It helps my concentration	☐
It keeps my weight down	☐
It helps me socialise	☐
It helps to control pain	☐

Let's now go through each of the reasons you might have given for smoking, and see what other smokers said.

I enjoy it

In fact only 50 per cent of smokers report that they enjoy smoking. Young smokers enjoy it *less* than older smokers, and women enjoy it less than men.

Now here's something to think about. You may be surprised to learn that how much you enjoy smoking is not linked to how addicted you are to cigarettes. It will make no difference to your chances of lasting success at stopping. Enjoyment of smoking may put some people off trying to quit, but when you get to the point where you are going to have a go at stopping, enjoyment is no longer part of the picture.

I'm not saying you won't miss your cigarettes, and won't feel a twinge of pleasure at the thought of smoking – especially when you see a friend lighting up or smell tobacco. But the research tells us that this will not be your main barrier to lasting success.

r e s e a r c h

The smell of tobacco: aroma or stink?

For some people the smell of tobacco is a sweet aroma, and for others it is a dreadful stink. When smokers are in the process of stopping, some detest the smell of cigarettes and actively avoid smoke from other people's cigarettes; others lift their noses and draw in the scent of tobacco, thoroughly enjoying the sensation.

You might imagine that the second group would be more likely to go back to smoking. My colleagues at the Royal London Hospital wanted to find out. So they asked more than 1,000 smokers who were attending their NHS Stop Smoking Service (one of the best in the world – see Chapter 8) about their reactions to the smell of smoke as they were trying to quit.

And guess what? Just over half of this group trying to stop smoking said they found the smell of other people's smoke pleasant, however it made *not the slightest bit of difference* to their chances of staying off cigarettes.

It helps me cope with stress

About 40 per cent of smokers say smoking helps them deal with stress. Women tend to give this reason more than men, and younger smokers give it more than older smokers.

Do you think smoking helps you cope with stress? If so, let me give you some facts and see what you think after that.

- **Fact 1**: Smokers report higher levels of stress than people who have never smoked.

- **Fact 2**: When smokers stop, after about a week they report their levels of stress going *down*, not up.

- **Fact 3**: If they start smoking again, their stress levels go back up again.

- **Fact 4**: If you put people who don't normally smoke in a stressful situation and give them nicotine, their stress levels go up, not down.

- **Fact 5**: Drugs that reduce anxiety do not help smokers to stop.

It seems to me that smoking is actually causing stress, not helping with it. So why are so many smokers convinced that smoking is helping them cope?

What I think is happening is this. We know that after a couple of hours of not smoking, your brain starts to miss its nicotine fix. You get edgy, restless and you start to feel a bit down. Your brain has got used to nicotine and is now experiencing withdrawal symptoms because your nicotine levels are falling. Then you have a cigarette and 'aaaah' – blessed relief! So you think that smoking has helped with stress, when all it has done is to restore you to where you would have been if you had not smoked.

I hope I have convinced you that smoking has merely tricked you into thinking it's helping with stress. There are plenty of other ways of tackling stress that actually do work.

Smoking's effect on your heart rate

By the way, when you quit smoking there are also some physical symptoms we measure in our studies that you wouldn't notice yourself. One of these is that your heart rate (pulse) goes down. On average, it goes down by about eight beats per minute.

In the first study I ever did on smoking, we measured smokers' heart rates before they stopped and up to ten days afterwards. These were heavy smokers and the average drop in heart rate was actually 15 beats per minute. We also drew blood so that we could measure their blood nicotine levels and concentrations of various other chemicals that are related to stress, such as adrenaline and cortisol. A lot of doctors think that your adrenaline levels increase when you stop smoking – because they see stopping as stressful – but in fact they go down. Nicotine raises your adrenaline output, and when you take the nicotine away, it goes down.

You can monitor your own heart rate by taking your pulse. You might have learnt how to do this at school. It is very simple and worth doing. When you stop smoking, you will be able to tell the difference.

To take your pulse, you simply need to:

1 Get a watch or clock with a second hand. If you have a watch on, take it off. You are going to time 30 seconds.
2 Put your left arm out, palm up. Take the first two fingers of your right hand and place them quite lightly on your left wrist as shown in the picture – pressing down just a little. Move your fingers around until you feel the pulse.
3 Count the number of times the pulse occurs over a 30-second interval.
4 Now double that number. That is your pulse rate.

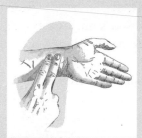

Fig 1.1 Taking your pulse

Your pulse rate will probably be around 80 beats per minute. It's unlikely to be less than 60 (unless you are pretty fit) or more than 90.

When you stop smoking it will almost certainly go down – quite a bit.

I am addicted to cigarettes

Almost 40 per cent of smokers report feeling addicted. Middle-aged smokers feel most addicted; there is no difference between the sexes.

Now if there was one thing you would think would be a barrier to quitting smoking, it is feeling addicted. You would think it would stop you from even trying to quit because you don't think you will succeed, and it should make you go back to smoking more quickly because, well, you are addicted!

Well, let me tell you that, according to my research, feeling addicted does not put smokers off trying to stop. In fact, if anything, it makes them more likely to have a go. When you think about it, perhaps that is not so surprising. No one likes to think that they are addicts, and breaking free from addiction is, after all, the point of this book.

I can also tell you that feeling addicted does not mean that you will actually find it harder to stop. If you feel addicted, you have just as good a chance of stopping as anyone else. Feeling addicted and being addicted are not the same thing at all. So take heart!

research

Medical students and exams

I used to teach medical students and, for my sins, I was put in charge of what was called 'study skills' – basically my job was to help the students pass their exams.

One year I did a little experiment: I asked students at the beginning of their first year of study to rate how likely they thought they were to pass the exams at the end of the year. Some were very confident and some really thought they would struggle. When the end of the year came, I compared their marks with what they had predicted at the start of the year. Guess what? There was no relationship whatsoever!

I used this information to good effect in future years, and – most importantly – I told those who were anxious about failing that they had just as good a chance as their more confident friends.

And my research tells me the same thing with stopping smoking. Don't worry if you think you stand very little chance. The truth is that you stand just as good a chance as anyone else. And if you follow the advice in this book – you'll have a much better chance!

It gives me something to do

Relief from boredom is mentioned by about 20 per cent of smokers when asked why they light up. This seems to be particularly important for young smokers.

When you think about it, it's a bit odd that smoking should be seen as 'giving you something to do'. It's not as though smoking is particularly, well … interesting. But the fact is that the nicotine from your cigarettes fools your brain into thinking you are actually 'doing' something useful.

Is smoking really 'doing something'?

A lot of people think that it is the actions of smoking – holding the cigarette, putting it to your lips, sucking on it – that are keeping boredom at bay, but you only have to try a little experiment to see that this isn't true . . .

Unless you have already stopped smoking, the next time you are bored and feel like lighting up, puff on the cigarette just as you would if you were smoking, but *don't light it*.

Not only will you feel a bit of a twit, you'll see that it really doesn't do the business when it comes to dealing with the boredom. You might even find that it makes you more bored.

It helps my concentration

About ten per cent of smokers say they smoke to help with concentration. To be honest, I was surprised when I got this finding from my research. I would have thought it would be more – it is certainly the case that a lack of ability to concentrate is something that a lot of smokers report when they can't smoke for a while. Older smokers report this more than younger smokers, and men report it more than women.

The tobacco industry has gone to some lengths to persuade people that smoking helps with concentration and memory. And they succeeded in persuading quite a lot of us that it does – including some eminent researchers. But the reality is that if there is such an effect, it is very weak. On the other hand, if you are a regular smoker and can't smoke for a while, you are likely to find it hard to keep your attention focused.

So what is going on? Well, within a couple of hours of not smoking you will start to experience nicotine-withdrawal symptoms. One of these is difficulty concentrating. You then smoke a cigarette and it brings you back to normal.

You can see what's happening here – it's just like with stress. Smoking doesn't really help you concentrate – it just seems to. Your powers of concentration are no different from what they would be if you had never smoked. It's just that your brain has got used to its nicotine fix. So you have the illusion that smoking helps you concentrate, when in fact it's just staving off withdrawal symptoms that wouldn't exist without cigarettes.

It keeps my weight down

You may be surprised to learn that only about ten per cent of smokers report this as a reason for smoking. There are more women than men, but still not many.

If you have tried to stop before, the chances are that you will have put on weight. It is extremely common. The reason is that nicotine does two things to keep you a bit thinner: it reduces your appetite and it speeds up your metabolism.

Eating more when you stop smoking has nothing at all to do with any 'oral' fixation or wanting to put something in your mouth. One of the first studies I did on smoking involved switching smokers to a very low nicotine cigarette. This meant they were getting all the oral satisfaction they could handle, but they still experienced an increase in hunger. By the way, they also started to experience chest pains – from the effort of dragging on the cigarettes to get something out of them!

Another reason we know that the increased appetite has got nothing to do with oral fixation is that nicotine patches help reduce the increase in appetite when smokers stop – even though (when used according to the manufacturers' instructions and placed on the skin rather than chewed) they don't get anywhere near the mouth.

So the big question is: how much of a barrier is this to stopping smoking? Here's the funny thing. Smokers who report that they smoke for weight control are actually *more* likely to try to stop and more likely to succeed! This seems strange to me, just as it must to you. I know people who specifically said they went back to smoking because they had gained weight. Perhaps you have.

I guess, for the majority of smokers trying to give up, dieting to avoid gaining weight puts them at greater risk of relapse to smoking than feeling bad about the weight they gain. Trying to diet at the same time as stopping smoking might be just too much to cope with.

Let me give you a couple of positive messages. First of all, I want to reassure you: the effect on your health of this weight gain will be more than offset by the benefit from not inhaling cigarette smoke. Secondly, if you put into practice some of the ideas in this book about stopping smoking, they could stand you in very good stead when it comes to losing weight.

It helps me socialise

Smoking is often thought of as a sociable activity. But in fact only around ten per cent of smokers report that socialising is one of the reasons they smoke. And it is a much bigger deal for young smokers than older smokers. People who smoke for social reasons don't find it any harder (or easier) to stop than others.

We don't always like to admit it, but sometimes it's good to feel part of a 'crowd' – people we connect with, people we have some-thing in common with. This can be especially true now that smokers are in a small minority and often report feeling like a persecuted underclass. You can stand or sit around and chat with people on breaks. You can exchange the gifts of the cigarette and the light. Although I'm going to advise you to stay away from these kinds of situations, at least for a while, the camaraderie of smoking does not have to be a barrier to quitting: there are ways of dealing with the friendly offer of a cigarette.

It helps to control pain

Pain relief is definitely a factor for some smokers: about five per cent of you – much more for older than younger smokers.

For a long time we never asked smokers about whether they smoked for pain relief, even though there were studies showing that nicotine reduces pain in other animals. What put me on to this was a study done by one of my students in Ghana. Over there, it is quite common for people to smoke and chew tobacco to relieve pain – particularly from toothache. That got me thinking about whether it would be true in this country.

Actually, nicotine has long been known to have pain-relieving properties. Smoking rates are very high in people who suffer from chronic pain. The problem is that I suspect (though I don't know) that it really isn't helping and may even be making things worse. That is because I think that, just like with other painkillers, our bodies get used to the nicotine and it no longer has the desired effect.

What's really keeping you smoking?

So those are the most common reasons people give for smoking. My guess is that several of them will apply to you. Now, let me tell you something: *the things that matter most in keeping you smoking are not on that list*.

Let me explain. I will start with the short version and then, for those of you who are interested, I will give you the longer version. Here goes.

Why it is hard to stop smoking: the short version

You smoke because the nicotine you have been inhaling for all those years has changed your brain chemistry to create powerful *urges to smoke*.

The urges come about because every puff on a cigarette sends a rapid nicotine 'hit' to the part of your brain that makes you do things, *without you having to feel any pleasure from the experience or gain any benefit*. These urges are triggered because nicotine has trained the part of your brain that gets you to do things to light up a cigarette whenever you find yourself in a situation where you would normally smoke.

That is as short as I can make it. So what does this mean for you and how you quit?

First, it means that no blame whatsoever can be attached to you because you find it difficult to stay off cigarettes. On the contrary, continuing to battle with it despite the difficulty is in my view a sign of real strength.

Secondly, it means stopping smoking involves doing everything you can to avoid, reduce and cope with the urges to smoke – and you can do a lot.

Thirdly, despite what some people claim – you are almost certainly going to need to use your *willpower* at some point. Whether it's hanging on by your fingernails or resisting the little voice that says, 'Go on! One won't hurt you,' you will have to show self-control. You are going to have to stop yourself smoking when your brain is telling you to smoke. At times like these, you have to care more about not taking that dreaded puff than anything else. And each time you exert self-control and fight off the urge to smoke, you are making progress. You are climbing another rung of the ladder out of the hole that smoking has dug for you.

Finally, it means that medicines that reduce the urges to smoke and the withdrawal symptoms will help you stay stopped. These may be nicotine products, such as nicotine skin patches, nicotine gum, nicotine lozenges and so on, or they may be pills, such as Champix or Zyban, that your doctor can prescribe. These medicines are safe and effective. They are not a magic cure, and you still need willpower, but they will make quitting easier by reducing the smoking urges.

Now here's the longer version of why it's hard to stop smoking. Feel free to skip ahead to 'Smoking situations' on page 38, but I hope you find this interesting.

Nicotine's effect on your brain

Imagine the brain as a complex web of nerve cells. For us to think, feel, eat and even breathe, these nerve cells need to talk to each other. They do this by sending chemicals back and forth as messengers – these are called 'neurotransmitters'. These neurotransmitters are essential to all brain activity – all our thoughts and feelings, and also the work the brain does that we are not aware of, like controlling our breathing.

Nicotine is like a cuckoo in the nest. To our brains, it looks like one of these chemical messengers that nerve cells use to communicate with each other. This chemical is called 'acetylcholine'. (Don't worry, I'm not going to test you on these names later!) It was actually the first neurotransmitter to be discovered.

When you inhale nicotine in cigarette smoke, it is absorbed into the bloodstream through the massive surface area of the lungs (about the size of a tennis court). Because nicotine is absorbed over such a large surface area it gets into your bloodstream very quickly. So each puff on a cigarette gives you a rapid 'nicotine hit' to the brain.

There is a particular part of the brain, deep down, very near the centre, which we often call the 'central reward pathway'. Its job is to get you to do things that are useful to you in situations when you need to do them. When something that our brain considers valuable or useful happens, 'receptors' on the nerve cells at the start of the pathway take up the chemical messenger acetylcholine. This causes another chemical messenger, dopamine, to be released at the other end of it which acts as a kind of reward.

We know from a huge number of studies that this release of dopamine is how humans learn to do things that help with our survival, such as finding food and having sex. When the reward pathway is activated, it makes your brain pay attention to whatever you were just doing and the situation in which you were doing it; then when you find yourself in the same situation again, your brain creates the impulse to do it again.

The way the brain links this impulse to do something with situations in which it is rewarded is a process that psychologists call 'positive reinforcement'. It is how you train a dog to sit up and beg for food or treats.

However, it is not just useful things that can activate your brain's reward pathway. In the case of smoking, your brain is being taught to sit up and beg for nicotine.

Your nicotine hit hijacks the reward system by pretending to be acetylcholine. It activates the central reward pathway and releases dopamine when all you have done is puff on a cigarette. So, as far as your brain is concerned, smoking a cigarette is a bit like eating food when you are hungry, drinking when you are thirsty, telling a funny joke, getting satisfaction from a job well done or having sex … *not* because it is so brilliantly enjoyable but simply because it activated the brain pathway which tells you to do it again.

And you don't have to feel anything when this happens. You can be blissfully ignorant of what is going on. It is all automatic. It takes place in the animal part of your brain outside your awareness. And this animal part will learn to create an impulse to smoke again when you are in the same situations.

I want to take the liberty of saying this again in another way – because it goes so much against common opinion that I find people

Our animal and human brains

Humans appeared very recently in the history of the earth. In our present form we evolved less than a million years ago from creatures much like today's apes. And these creatures evolved from creatures a lot like today's other mammals.

What this means is that a lot of our bodies are very similar to those of other mammals. That is why drugs are usually tested on other animals before they are allowed to be tested on humans. We share almost all the same organs as creatures as lowly as the rat. Unfortunately for rats, that makes them quite useful as guinea pigs! (And as for guinea pigs ...)

When it comes to our brains, we have a lot in common with rats, dogs, cats, monkeys and so on. That 'animal' part of our brain has remained fairly similar to what it was like before we became humans.

When we acquired the ability to talk things really took off for us. Our animal brain was only able to react to what is going on at the time – hunger, thirst, pleasure, pain etc. – but our human brain was able to work things out and plan quite a long way ahead. It allowed us to decide what we *should* do and not just react to what we *want* or *need* to do.

Nicotine attacks the animal part of our brains: the part that has a 220 million-year head start on the clever part of our brains that can talk and tell us what we really should or should not do. Nicotine makes the animal part of your brain badger the conscious 'you' to light up.

When the human part of your brain decides that you shouldn't smoke – somehow you have to overpower this animal force. (I'll be looking at how you can do this in the next chapter.)

don't always get it the first time. What I am saying is: despite how it may seem to you, it is *not* your enjoyment of smoking that is stopping you from quitting. The nicotine hit you get from each puff on a cigarette simply creates the *impulse* to smoke whenever you find yourself in a situation where you would normally light up. It does this by attaching itself to the receptors in your animal brain, causing nerve pathways to fire, which in turn causes dopamine to be released in the brain. It is this dopamine release that attaches the impulse to smoke to whatever situation you happen to be in when you normally do it.

That is one reason why, even though you may be a heavy smoker, you mostly do not feel the urge to light up in situations where you are not allowed to smoke, such as supermarkets. If you cannot smoke in these situations, your brain has not made those connections.

Smoking situations

So situations are crucial in your urges to smoke, and it is likely that when you come to stop there will be times and places where you may expect to experience a strong impulse to smoke.

Opposite is a list of those in which you might find yourself feeling the urge to smoke. Go through the list and see how many of these apply to you.

I'll come back to these situations in Chapter 13, when looking at ways to avoid temptation. But you might be interested to hear what other smokers say. I commissioned a household survey of a representative sample of just over 700 adult smokers in England. The table on page 40 gives the percentage of smokers who selected each of the situations listed.

Obviously the responses will depend on how often the smokers in the sample were in each of the situations listed – for example, many of them might not read very much, or drive. But the results give you an idea as to what the high-risk situations are likely to be.

Getting hooked

If you smoke ten cigarettes a day for ten years, and you take an average of ten puffs on each cigarette, you will have taken in the region of 365,000 puffs and got 365,000 hits. Each hit trains you to smoke. That is a lot of training.

But you don't need 365,000 hits. The brain starts to adapt to nicotine very quickly. Teenagers who have been smoking for just a few months already take in as much nicotine from each cigarette as adults, and when they try to stop they experience the same urges to smoke and find it just as difficult.

Some of my colleagues believe that even smoking a single cigarette changes the brain profoundly to make it start to need to smoke. They may be right. Dr Jenny Fidler who used to be in my team at University College London reported a study a few years ago which showed that just having smoked one cigarette dramatically increased a teenager's chances of becoming a regular smoker years later – *even if they didn't smoke another cigarette for over a year*. Something in their brains had changed so they were vulnerable to situations later in their lives that would trigger the desire to smoke.

Do you often smoke in the following situations?
(Pick as many answers as you like)

1	Just after waking in the morning	☐
2	Just before going to sleep in the evening	☐
3	During the night	☐
4	During meals	☐
5	After meals	☐
6	While driving	☐
7	While walking	☐
8	While waiting for a bus or train	☐
9	While working	☐
10	While doing housework at home	☐
11	When taking a break	☐
12	When drinking alcohol	☐
13	When drinking coffee or tea	☐
14	While doing nothing in particular	☐
15	While watching TV or videos	☐
16	When using a computer at home	☐
17	When reading	☐
18	While listening to the radio	☐
19	While out at a concert/theatre/cinema	☐
20	While out at a restaurant	☐
21	When at a bar or pub	☐

Do you often smoke in the following situations?		Percentage selecting this response
1	Just after waking in the morning	29%
2	Just before going to sleep in the evening	26%
3	During the night	10%
4	During meals	3%
5	After meals	56%
6	While driving	17%
7	While walking	21%
8	While waiting for a bus or train	14%
9	While working or studying	15%
10	While doing housework at home	12%
11	When taking a break	35%
12	When drinking alcohol	43%
13	When drinking coffee or tea	35%
14	While doing nothing in particular	26%
15	While watching TV or videos	24%
16	When using a computer at home	12%
17	When reading	10%
18	While listening to the radio	13%
19	While out at a concert/theatre/cinema	25%
20	While out at a restaurant	12%
21	When at a bar or pub	30%

If you wanted to design a chemical that would take over your brain and get you using it again and again, even when you didn't enjoy it and wanted to stop, you could hardly do better than nicotine.

Nicotine hunger

So far, I've told you that when you find yourself in a situation where you would normally smoke, nicotine has trained one part of your brain to send a signal to another part saying: 'smoke!'

That is why you can go a long time without smoking and not feel the need for a cigarette, but when you find yourself in a situation where you would usually smoke, you suddenly get the urge to light up. And in situations where you have never smoked, perhaps a long plane journey, you can feel okay – until you land …

But there is more. Inhaling cigarette smoke makes you hungry for nicotine. Not all smokers experience this, but a lot get this feeling I call 'nicotine hunger'. When nicotine levels in the brain fall below a certain level, they feel a 'drive' which is very similar to hunger for food, but in this case it is for nicotine.

What happens is that the brain pathway I talked about earlier stops working properly unless it is topped up with nicotine. When the nicotine levels drop, there is too little dopamine being produced and you feel a kind of gnawing emptiness. You can reduce this by taking in nicotine, for example from a nicotine patch.

So, quite apart from the fact that nicotine triggers the urge to smoke in situations where you would normally smoke, it also creates a kind of 'nicotine hunger' when levels in the brain get low.

But there's more … to make matters worse you start to feel a whole load of unpleasant symptoms when you can't smoke.

Nicotine-withdrawal symptoms

Nicotine withdrawal can affect you in many ways. Many smokers report feeling irritable and unable to concentrate over the first few weeks after quitting, and some feel anxious, depressed and unable to sleep. There is also an array of physical symptoms that you might have, including constipation and mouth sores.

Most of the unpleasant nicotine-withdrawal symptoms last only one to four weeks. The only one that lasts longer is hunger. And by that I mean hunger for food. This typically keeps going for about three months.

The hunger is mainly for foods that are rich in 'carbohydrates' – sweets, cakes and that kind of thing. People used to think that this hunger was because smokers missed the regular habit of putting something in their mouth. But, as I mentioned a bit earlier, we have known since the 1980s that isn't true. It's totally down to nicotine.

r e s e a r c h

Nicotine withdrawal: The train study

About ten years ago I helped run a study, led by my friend and colleague Professor Peter Hajek (founder of the model of group support given to smokers right across the globe), to find out how long it takes before smokers start to feel symptoms of nicotine withdrawal when they cannot smoke.

We took a group of smokers and put them on a train from London to Glasgow. During the journey they were not able to smoke. We then measured how they felt every 30 minutes during the four-hour journey. This was the first study anyone had ever done to see how quickly nicotine-withdrawal symptoms and urges to smoke emerged in a natural setting, outside the laboratory.

We found that the mood of our volunteers started to deteriorate quite quickly, and within about 90 minutes we could definitely tell that they were starting to feel the pinch. They were also starting to feel urges to smoke. Things continued to get progressively worse over the course of the train journey.

When the train reached Glasgow, our volunteers couldn't wait to get off the train and light up. In the space of just four hours, they had gone from pretty calm and relaxed to jittery, irritable and generally not too happy.

And then our intrepid volunteers were put on a train to Edinburgh where they spent the night and we made them go through the whole thing again on the train back to London!

The results were clear on both journeys: nicotine-withdrawal symptoms come on very quickly and they are not pleasant. It is slightly worrying to think that the person driving your bus or flying your plane may be feeling distracted and irritable on a long journey.

On the following page is a quick questionnaire that my research team uses to measure nicotine hunger and nicotine-withdrawal symptoms. The smokers in our studies fill in the questionnaire while they are still smoking and then again at various points after they have stopped. All of these symptoms typically get worse for a while and then get better again – for some symptoms, better than while you were smoking.

If you want to see how your own quit attempt is going, try filling in this questionnaire now, then try again every day after you have stopped for a week, and then once a week for a month. It's a good way of charting your progress.

I will come back to this when talking about the ingredients that will make up your formula because there is a lot you can do to reduce these symptoms.

So in a nutshell … nicotine keeps you smoking because:

1 The nicotine hit creates a link in your brain between situations in which you smoke and the impulse to light up.
2 For some of you – particularly if you are the kind of smoker who has to smoke first thing in the morning – you start to experience a gnawing 'nicotine hunger' when concentrations of nicotine in your brain fall below a certain level.
3 When your brain nicotine concentrations fall below a given level you start to experience nicotine-withdrawal symptoms such as irritability and difficulty concentrating.

So it's not surprising then that even powerful figures such as President Obama struggle to resist the pull back to smoking. It is so easy just to give in and say to yourself that you'll try again on another day – or that 'one won't hurt'…

Mood and physical symptoms scale questionnaire

1. Please show for each of the items below how you have been feeling over the past 24 hours. *(Circle one number for each item).*

	Not at all	Slightly	Somewhat	Very	Extremely
Depressed	1	2	3	4	5
Anxious	1	2	3	4	5
Irritable	1	2	3	4	5
Restless	1	2	3	4	5
Hungry	1	2	3	4	5
Poor concentration	1	2	3	4	5
Poor sleep at night	1	2	3	4	5

2. Have you experienced any of the following over the past 24 hours?
(Circle one number for each item).

	No	Slight	Moderate	Severe	Very severe
Sores in the mouth	1	2	3	4	5
Constipation	1	2	3	4	5
Cough/sore throat	1	2	3	4	5

3. How much of the time have you felt the urge to smoke in the past 24 hours?
(Circle one number)

Not at all	A little of the time	Some of the time	A lot of the time	Almost all of the time	All the time
1	2	3	4	5	6

4. How strong have the urges to smoke been?
(Circle one number)

No urges	Slight	Moderate	Strong	Very strong	Extremely strong
1	2	3	4	5	6

Chapter 2

The Psychology of Smoking – and How you Can Use it to Stop

From what I've said so far it might look as though I think that smoking is only about nicotine and that we humans are not very different from laboratory rats. Let me correct that impression.

Without nicotine you would not smoke – but of course there is much more to it than that. Think of nicotine as the acorn from which the oak tree of addiction grows. No acorn – no tree. But it takes a lot more than an acorn to grow a mighty oak tree.

Why we do what we do

Let's start with perhaps the most basic question: what makes us do anything? For example, why are you reading this book? And, equally important, on the opposite side: what makes us *not* do things? For example, why are you not wearing a tutu? (I'm assuming you aren't, though by the law of averages, if this book sells well, perhaps at least one of you will be!)

In a way, the answer is very simple: everything we do is the result of a battle between our impulses and inhibitions.

Impulses drive our actions and inhibitions stop us doing things.

For example, you see someone smoking and you have an impulse to light up, but you are in a restaurant so you stop yourself.

Some of these impulses and inhibitions are unconscious, like breathing or stopping in your tracks when startled. Or they stem from a basic desire for things our brains expect to make us feel good, like going to the cinema. Some people think of this as the *emotional part* of our brain, while others call it 'automatic'.

You might think of impulses as things that don't involve any thought, but actually everything we do involves impulses in the end. So while some impulses come from our instincts and desire, others stem from our conscious beliefs about what would be the correct thing to do: what is right and wrong, harmful or beneficial, good or bad, appropriate or not appropriate – what we think will lead to a positive or negative outcome. And so do some inhibitions – refraining from reaching for a cream bun, or a cigarette. Some people call this the *rational part* of our brain.

What we are talking about here is what people refer to as the head and the heart. But I think it is more accurate to talk about your animal and human brain.

Our minds – our lives – are controlled by the interplay of these two forces: automatic processes, which produce our wants and needs, and our conscious decisions on what we think is a good idea. And these forces can work with or against each other.

Breathing is an instinct, and most of the time you don't pay any attention to it. But if you want to hold your breath for a while, or breathe faster, you can.

If I puff air into your eye, you blink; that is an instinct. Unless you are very good at self-control, you can't stop yourself – even if you want to. But you can quite easily force yourself to blink. And in a staring contest with a friend you can stop yourself blinking – at least for a while.

You see a delicious-looking dessert you want to eat, but you are on a diet and you have already eaten quite a big meal so you know you shouldn't – so you restrain yourself.

You have drunk a couple of pints of beer or glasses of wine at a party and you are offered some more. This would take you over your personal limit – but you go ahead and drink anyway.

You normally go to the gym for a workout on Saturday mornings, but when you wake up you don't feel like it – so you lie in.

You have stopped smoking because you don't want to get sick and die from lung cancer, but nicotine hunger is gnawing away at you, so you need a cigarette.

It's just after a meal when you would normally smoke, so the urge to smoke is even greater, and you are feeling stressed after a hard day at work, which makes things even worse … but you have decided not to smoke, so you don't.

These tug of war matches play out consciously and unconsciously all the time. As you read this there has been a tug of war between continuing to read and getting up and doing something else. If the phone rings, you will probably put this book down and answer it. But if the book is gripping enough, you might ignore it!

Displacement reactions: the three-spined stickleback

My favourite subject at school was biology. I had a wonderful teacher called Hank Robinson, and one of his lessons has stuck in my mind all these years. We were told the story of the three-spined stickleback.

Fig 2.1 A three-spined stickleback

Imagine a three-spined stickleback happily swimming along, minding its own business. Suddenly it spots another three-spined stickleback coming towards it. It isn't sure what to do. Part of it wants to attack it. The other part wants to swim away as quickly as possible. It doesn't have long to decide, and the other fish is getting closer. So what does it do?

It digs a hole!

Digging the hole is what is called a 'displacement reaction'. This is when the mental tug of war between going forward and back creates an energy that has to express itself somehow, and the way it does this is by doing something else entirely.

And that's often what humans do when we're faced with conflicting emotions. For example, we might scratch our heads, rub our hands, squirm in a chair, clear our throat, sniff, ruffle our hair, stroke our chin, grind our teeth …

If you are sitting down while reading this you will have been shifting your position all the time to keep comfortable. You may have cleared your throat a few times, scratched your nose … and so on.

Look closely at people on the bus or in cafes or anywhere where they are sitting down. They are almost never still. The tug of war that goes on at the automatic and conscious level is keeping them moving, looking around, sniffing, fidgeting, yawning…

Now let's look a bit more closely at these forces of motivation. The reason for doing this is to help you understand what is driving your desire to smoke and what you need to do to give yourself strength to resist.

Instinct

When we do things without thinking it is very often because we react emotionally; we react out of reflex or we just imitate what we see someone else do. These are instinctive responses and we don't have to learn them. They are wired into our brains. Something really bad happens and we cry; someone raises a fist to us and we flinch; we run short of oxygen, we breathe harder; something tickles our nose and we sneeze.

A lot of the time we can stop ourselves doing things instinctively. That is much of what growing up is about. We learn not to grab for things we want, cry when we are hurt, lash out when we are angry.

But a lot of time we can't – or we don't. We react instinctively and sometimes live to regret it.

Habit

While instincts are wired into our brain, habits have to be learned. From our very first waking moment we are learning habits that will enable us to do things we need to do in order to survive. Most of our actions are like this. We can't be thinking about every little thing all the time. We need to be able to concentrate on the big stuff.

We learn habits by doing things and being either rewarded or punished in little ways.

A baby reaches for something it wants to grab; when it succeeds it is rewarded and so learns automatic control of its movements. We learn that a switch just to the right of the bathroom door turns the light on, and so we learn automatically to reach for the switch as we go in.

Habits are the building blocks of behaviour. Most of the time we are not aware of them – we just know what we want to achieve and, lo and behold, our brains put together the habits that make it happen. The more often we do something and get rewarded for it, the stronger the habit becomes.

Does this sound familiar? Nicotine provides just this kind of reward. People talk about smoking as a 'bad habit'. In this sense that is absolutely right. It is a habit that you learn because nicotine tricks the brain into thinking it is doing something useful when you smoke.

Now if habits are not rewarded, they 'extinguish'. If you press the light switch and nothing happens, eventually you stop reaching for it automatically (or call the electrician!).

So if you didn't get any reward from nicotine, your smoking habit would extinguish. That is the idea behind a new approach to stopping smoking that I will mention later in the Appendix: the nicotine vaccine. It doesn't figure in the list of ingredients because at the moment it is still just something that is being tried out. But drug companies are investing hundreds of millions of pounds in trying to find a vaccine that will stop nicotine getting to the brain – and if they achieve that we could see the end of smoking forever. But don't hold your breath …

Wants

Instincts and habits happen without us thinking about it. But of course a lot of our behaviour involves us trying to get something or avoid something.

If I mention the word 'chocolate', it conjures up an image and memories of what it tastes like. The chances are that you will now feel that you would like to experience the pleasure of eating some – at least a little bit. Now you may not have any chocolate nearby and, since you are engrossed in my lesson in psychology, you may not feel like going out to get some. Unless you are hungry and the idea of chocolate is beginning to take hold in your mind …

So we go through our lives having images of things conjured up by the world around us and our memories. And if these images are of things we might be able to get our hands on, we experience this feeling of 'wanting'.

What can make us want things? Lots of things, from drives, such as hunger and thirst, to a desire for status, self-respect, money, comfort, love, etc. – basically anything that we expect to give us pleasure, comfort or satisfaction for whatever reason. Most of us don't take time to stop and think about what gives us pleasure and sometimes we just go with the flow, or what's expected, and don't think about whether we really enjoy it.

When I was first at university it took me a year to discover I didn't really like staying up all night and partying – I liked sitting at home watching TV, maybe chatting with a friend and especially sleeping!

Getting to know what truly gives you pleasure is a very important lesson in life. Sometimes pleasure and pain are hard to disentangle. As a child I was hooked on making plastic models of ships, aircraft, cars, tanks and so on. Each week I'd take my pocket money and I can still feel the excitement and anticipation I felt going into the model shop. Then I'd get my new model home and couldn't wait to get started making it.

But it rarely went smoothly. The bits wouldn't fit together like they should, and my impatience would get the better of me, so I'd make a mess of it and sometimes would get really angry – hunched over the kitchen table with bits of plastic strewn over it, cursing away. My mother would say, 'I don't know why you keep buying those models – they just make you angry.' But there was something that kept me hooked. I guess most of the time I managed to get past the anger and frustration and produce something that gave me a sense of achievement.

What am I saying here? Wants are not always simple. Sometimes we think we want things but actually they don't give us pleasure. And sometimes we want things even though they give us pain. Does that sound familiar?

Needs

Wants are all about anticipated pleasure, comfort or satisfaction. Needs, on the other hand, are all about relief: relief from pain and from mental and physical discomfort.

Attachment to cigarettes and feelings of bereavement

We become attached to things and people who are 'there for us' – parents, close friends, siblings. They reward us and meet our needs. They make us feel good. We like being with them. They are part of our lives. We can't imagine life without them.

For a lot of smokers, cigarettes are like that. You get attached to them. They are part of your life. And what I hear a lot from smokers who stop is that they experience a strong sense of bereavement – like they have lost a close friend.

To a non-smoker this sounds silly. How can you become attached to chopped tobacco rolled up in a piece of paper that you put to your lips and set fire to?

The answer is that your animal brain can't tell the difference between nicotine from a cigarette and a smile from a loved one. As far as it's concerned, it's all pretty much the same. So your animal brain is naturally going to get attached to this constant source of reward.

When you don't smoke, your animal brain feels bad – it misses its nicotine hit. It thinks its loved one has gone away. And when you tell your brain that its friend has gone away forever to the great ashtray in the sky, naturally it is going to feel the loss.

You are sitting reading this book. Suddenly you become aware that you need to go to the toilet. At some point this feeling will reach a point where it makes you stop reading and head off to the bathroom.

Or you have an itch and you scratch it. Or you have a headache and you take an aspirin. Or you are worried about whether you left the gas on in the kitchen, so you go and check. Or you are lying on your back in bed and you become uncomfortable, so you change your position.

You get the idea. We have to distinguish between wants, which are linked to feeling good, and needs, which are linked to avoiding or stopping feeling bad.

And of course these things are closely tied to each other. A child sees an ice cream van and suddenly wants an ice cream – so badly that the thought of not getting the ice cream is unbearable – so the child cries and screams. Without knowing the context, one would be hard put to tell the difference between a picture of a young child crying because he can't get an ice cream and a child crying because of a tragedy that has befallen his parents.

For our animal brain, which is driving all of this, there isn't a great deal of difference. It is only as humans that we grow up to learn that some wants and needs have more significance and become imbued with dignity and tragedy.

Good and bad versus feeling good and bad

Everything I have talked about so far has involved our animal brain. With habits and instincts we react to events. With wants and needs we form images of things that make us feel good or bad and we go after them or avoid them.

Nicotine works directly on this part of your brain. It trains you to smoke as an automatic habit, and by making you want and need to smoke. Is that biology or is it psychology? The answer of course is that it is both.

But now comes the pure psychology. A few million years ago our ancestors learned to talk. Probably around the same time, they also learned to think about themselves – to form a self-identity.

If you have children you will remember (or will still be experiencing) how frustrating it can be trying to figure out what they want or need before they can talk. Does the nappy need changing? Are they hungry? Why on earth are they crying?

It is so much better when they can tell you what they want or need. Of course that too has its drawbacks, but being able to communicate our wants and needs is fundamental to satisfying each other – working as a team. And that needs language and a sense of self. (I realise that bees work very well as a team, and their language and sense of self are, shall we say, limited. But I'm talking about much more flexible and complex problem-solving abilities.) And with language and a sense of self comes a whole new way of representing the world that our animal cousins don't have. We can have 'beliefs'.

Beliefs are representations of the world that can be expressed through language. And a lot of our beliefs involve some sentiment of 'good' and 'bad'.

We learn early on from carers and teachers that some things are 'right' and 'wrong', 'harmful' or 'helpful', etc. We also learn that we are supposed to want and need things that are good, and avoid things that are bad. Knowing about good and bad gives us a huge advantage over other animals. We don't have to find out through experience whether something is going to be to our advantage – someone else can tell us, or we can work it out.

So you don't have to experience lung cancer to feel a need to avoid it; someone can tell you about it, and you can decide that it is a bad thing. This is incredibly useful, but there is a catch.

The catch is that just believing something is good is not in itself enough to make you want or need it – and believing it is bad is not enough to make you want or need to avoid it. Something has to connect these beliefs to your animal brain to make you *feel* something. Advertisers know this of course. There aren't too many advertisements which just list all the good things about a product – they use *imagery* to connect their product with your desires. The same is true for punchy government advertisements that encourage you to stop smoking, or pictures of gangrenous feet on cigarette packets.

So just knowing that smoking causes cancer, shortens your life by ten years and kills 5 million people each year is not necessarily going to make you feel strongly enough to make you stop. But if you cough up blood or have a heart attack – that is a different matter.

The trick, then, in getting our beliefs to control our behaviours is to find ways to make them mean something to us: to make us feel.

Planning

So as human beings we have the ability to *decide* what we think is good and bad, and as long as this makes us *feel* good or bad we will act on those beliefs. We can do this because we have the capacity for language and a sense of ourselves. This uniquely human capability also means that we can make plans. We don't just have to act in the here and now. We can decide on things that we will do in the future. We can form 'intentions'.

Intentions are vital to any kind of normal life. If you keep a diary of appointments, it is a record of your intentions. When you decide to go to work, you are making an intention. When you decide to go for lunch, you are making an intention. When you decide to stop smoking, you are making an intention.

Plans form the backbone of our lives. They give us purpose, structure and direction. And they allow us to function in a modern society, where certain things have to be done at certain times.

But – and it is a very big but – they do not have a hotline to our actions. If you think about it, it is obvious: a lot of things have to happen for your intentions to turn into action.

First, you have to remember them. I have always had a problem with remembering things I'm supposed to be doing, and it's getting worse as I get older. I was the proverbial absent-minded professor long before I was a professor. Fortunately, now that I am a professor people cut me more slack because it kind of comes with the job!

You will no doubt have had the experience of finding yourself going into a room to do something and then forgetting what it was. Believe it or not, I do hear of stories where people who have stopped smoking forget they have given up and light a cigarette.

Secondly, even if you remember your plan, it still has to be something you want to do. You might have gone off the idea. Perhaps you plan to go to a party, but when it comes to the day, you don't feel like it. You change your mind. There might be very good reasons to change your mind – perhaps the situation has changed and you don't need to do whatever it was you were planning after all. Or perhaps something else has come up that is a better idea. Or perhaps it is still a good idea but in all honesty you want or need to do something else more.

So for your plan to turn into action you have to remember it, still think it is a good idea and still want or need to do it more than you want or need to do something else.

So you decide to stop smoking. That is your plan. Then two hours into your quit attempt the nicotine hunger is beginning to kick in and you are experiencing the urges to smoke in situations where you used to smoke and, to cap it all, you are starting to feel a bit down. All this is because of the way that nicotine has rewired your animal brain. In that case, what is stopping you smoking?

Only your plan.

So you stick to your plan. Why? What is it that makes us stick to plans in the face of opposition? Two sets of things. One is the reason(s) you made the plan in the first place. If you still feel the same way about what you wanted or needed to do and nothing else has changed, there is no reason not to put the plan into effect. The other is commitment to the plan itself. The fact that you have made a plan is itself a source of wants and needs – as long as you are the kind of person who sticks to your plans.

Even if you can't remember exactly why you decided to do something – if you have made a definite plan, when the time comes you will be motivated to do it. This is very important for us, because we can't go around re-evaluating everything we do all the time – life's too short, and if you did that it would be a lot shorter!

But this is an area where people differ. You probably have a pretty good idea whether you are the kind of person who tends to stick to plans once you have made them. And if you are, you probably get frustrated with people who don't.

If there was ever a situation where you needed to be someone who sticks to plans it is when stopping smoking. Sometimes, the only thing that lies between you and that fatal puff is the fact that you have decided you will not smoke and that is all there is to it.

Age plays a role in this. As we get older, the research shows that we make fewer plans but when we make them we tend to stick to them. I think that this is one reason why young people try to stop more often than older people, but then more readily go back to smoking.

Identity and self-control

To recap: I have told you that a lot of our actions are automatic – either hard-wired instincts or learned habits. Our deliberate actions stem from feelings of wanting or needing something. I also said that there is a constant tug of war going on between different wants and needs and the result at each moment determines what we end up doing. Then I said that all this was going on in the animal part of our brain: the part that nicotine targets.

As humans, we have developed a sense of self and the capability for language. This means that we can form beliefs about things and reflect on our wants and needs. These beliefs allow us to plan ahead. But those plans still have to activate our wants and needs in the animal part of our brain to motivate us to act.

Now I want to continue this psychology lesson by looking more closely at what I think is our trump card when it comes to doing things that enable us to be successful in life – and in stopping smoking. It is called 'identity'.

There are lots of ways of thinking about identity. This is how *I* think about it …

Most of the time we are not thinking about ourselves – we look outward into the world and just get on with whatever it is we are doing. Most of the time while you have been reading this book, that is what you would be doing.

But now that I am talking about identity I have drawn your attention to you as a person and you have become self-aware. It is when you are self-aware that your identity can come into play in controlling how you behave.

Your identity is all those images, thoughts and feelings you have about yourself. What you think you look like, what kind of a person you are, what are your core values, your aspirations and so on. If I ask the question: 'Who and what are you?', your identity is the answers that come into your head.

Identity can be a massively powerful force driving our behaviour for good or ill. It makes mountain climbers, saints, prime ministers, suicide bombers, dictators, sporting heroes, scientists, musicians and actors. It also makes fathers, mothers, sons, daughters, vegetarians, runners, goths, punks, jazz fans, football supporters … And it also makes smokers and non-smokers.

So how does identity work? Two ways. One is that it can simply make you want to be something or someone so much that nothing else matters. You have no conflict – you just want to be a certain kind of person and that is all there is to it. The other is that it provides the driving force behind this thing we call 'self-control'.

I told you in the previous chapter that one thing that is almost certainly going to be needed to stop smoking is *self-control*. People often call it *willpower*. Some pundits claim that it is possible to stop smoking without it. But at some point you are going to be tempted to smoke and will have to resist that temptation. That is willpower.

Try this simple test. You will need a watch or clock with a second hand. When you've got one, take a deep breath in and see how long you can hold it. *Do it now…*

How long did you last? Ten seconds, thirty seconds, one minute, two minutes? However long you lasted, you could have gone longer. Nothing bad would happen to you until you'd gone several minutes.

In fact, almost all of us give in long before we come to any harm because the build-up of carbon dioxide in the blood triggers the urge to breathe. Professor Peter Hajek found that smokers who

Stopping smoking rarely happens by accident

Most smokers have to make a real effort to stop. This seems obvious, but it isn't to everybody. Here is case in point. A few years ago a drug company based in central Europe did a study of a medicine that is in fact quite effective at helping smokers to stop. The company was not very experienced at doing this kind of study. I was shown the results, and I was shocked to see that almost *no one* had stopped – not even for one day.

In all my years of doing this kind of research I had never seen anything like it. I probed the company representatives on what had happened. It was all very confusing until a thought struck me and I asked, 'You did actually tell the smokers they were supposed to stop, didn't you?' Puzzled frowns.

It had not occurred to them to mention it. I broke the silence. 'Then why did the smokers get involved in the first place?' They explained that the smokers got a free check-up as part of the study. Besides, why did the smokers need to know – the pill was supposed to make them stop, wasn't it?

But this is not how quitting works. The medicine was not designed to make the smokers stop just like that. It was designed to help them in combination with all the other stop-smoking ingredients they brought to the table – and to perhaps be the one that gave them the edge.

could hold their breath for longer succeeded in stopping smoking for longer – and this had nothing to do with their lungs not functioning as well. It was willpower.

How do you think of yourself? Are you a reluctant smoker? Would you be a reluctant non-smoker? In fact it doesn't matter particularly what kind of identity you will adopt as a non-smoker as long as you are very clear what it is, and that it does not involve smoking.

So what I am saying is that, yes, nicotine is a powerful source of wants and needs, but so too is identity. If identity can lead someone to risk his or her life to climb a mountain or walk to the South Pole, it can definitely overcome cigarette cravings. But you need to harness it – and by that I don't just mean developing your willpower. You need to build 'not smoking' into your core idea of yourself.

In Part Two, I'll give you some ideas for how to use your identity to support your quit attempt.

The power of resolve

You might just be familiar with a thing called the 'sensory homunculus'. It sounds like something from *The Lord of the Rings*. In fact, it's a model of how we would look if the size of each body part was in proportion to the amount of our brain devoted to processing information from that part.

So the hands and lips are enormous, because they form such a big part of our sensory experience, and the back of the head is rather less well developed! This is what it looks like:

Fig 2.2 The sensory homunculus

The human brain pays attention to things according to how important it thinks they are – *right now*. The word psychologists give to this is 'salience'. It is a very important word.

When you have just smoked your fifth cigarette of the evening at a party and your throat is sore, your mouth tastes like the bottom of a parrot's cage and your fingers are a rather unpleasant brown from the tar stains, you decide: that's it, it's time to stop smoking. What is 'salient' is everything that you hate about smoking. You are definitely going to stop. You have made a new 'personal rule'.

The new day dawns. You remember your resolve to stop smoking and look forward to your new life as an ex-smoker. You have breakfast. Still fine. You go to work. You miss the cigarette you would usually smoke at the bus stop. But still not too bad. Your personal rule is still 'salient'.

As the day wears on, your nicotine hunger starts to grow. Tea break comes and your workmates get up and head outside for the customary fag. Now the experience of last night is a faded memory, bleached of all those feelings that made you so sure you were going to stop. The fag beckons. Nicotine hunger is starting to bite.

What is keeping you from joining your workmates? Nothing … except your personal rule: 'I must not smoke'. You sensory homunculus has a massive great cigarette in its massive great hand and is wanting to draw it to its massive great lips! The personal rule is a tiny little voice in the back of a tiny little head.

So the six-hundred-million-dollar question is: how do you give the voice in your head a 1,000-watt amplifier and reduce the salience of the cigarette so that it's like you are looking at it through the wrong end of a telescope?

A huge part of this is how you set your *stop-smoking rule*.

You have probably found already that if your rule is, 'I'll *try* not to smoke' that isn't going to work. Just the same as, 'I'll *try* to lose weight' … The voice in your head just doesn't carry enough force. Why? Two reasons.

One is that there is no definite boundary, no 'box' around your behaviour – you can *try* not to smoke and still smoke. You can *try* to eat less and still eat whenever you feel like it! Secondly, it tells you what you are going to try to avoid but doesn't say anything about what you are going to do instead. So for your personal rule to shout down to the rest of your brain that smoking is not going to happen it must be *loud and clear*; it must *tell you what to do*.

The next thing is that your personal rule must really mean something to you. It is going to have to battle against your animal brain and have strong defences against the tricks that your animal brain will try to play. A vague concern about your health is not going to make it. Even panic about some health problem you've got right now won't cut it, because panic is not an emotion that can be kept up for long.

Health concern and panic are very good to start you off; so is being fed up with the cost of smoking. But to keep you going, a bigger change has to happen. A feeling that smoking is not something that forms part of your life any more.

This doesn't mean that you have to regret having smoked, or feel that smoking is disgusting – though that is a perfectly good approach. There are lots of ways of giving powerful emotional force to your no smoking rule, as I will describe in Part Two.

How to take control of your behaviour

The idea that there is an animal part of our brain and a human part has echoed through the ages in art and literature. In his wonderful book *The Happiness Hypothesis,* Jonathan Haidt talks about the 'rider and the elephant' as a metaphor from eastern philosophy; others talk about 'the rider and the horse' – as perhaps a more western metaphor.

The 'rider' is the human brain: capable of language, self-reflection, forming beliefs and making plans.

The 'horse' is our animal brain: responsible for our habits and instincts, our wants and needs, and generated by drives and emotions.

The rider and the horse have to find a way to communicate with each other, as the rider can only go where he or she wants by controlling the horse.

If you want to take control over your behaviour, you are going to have to 'strengthen the rider and tame the horse' (this phrase comes from an excellent article on the subject by Malte Friese and colleagues). Psychological science has taught us a lot about how to do this, and these lessons have been put to good effect to help people stop smoking, as you will see.

This is not a book on self-control, but I will tell you a few things that you should be able to use in your everyday life – and I will come back to these as ingredients of *The SmokeFree Formula* in Part Two.

Strengthening the rider

Here is a five-point plan for strengthening the rider:

1 **Set clear fixed rules:** You need to set clear-cut boundaries around what you can and cannot do. Once you have chosen your rules, you mustn't let yourself change them – so make sure they are realistic and doable. Imagine them carved in stone; whatever happens they can't be altered. Particularly helpful are ones that either say 'I never do this' or ones that are linked to specific situations, so 'When X happens, I always do Y'.

2 **Monitor and act accordingly:** You need to have good informa-

tion about how you're progressing towards your target. If things are going off track, you must have a clear idea about how to get back on track again. And if you are doing well, you need to make sure you are rewarded.

3 **Strengthen your new identity:** You need a strong idea about who and what you want to be. It is helpful to have a good role model if you can find one – but if you can't, then make one up in your head. It's about having a vision of being the person you want to be.

4 **Strengthen/extend your reasons for restraint:** The more reasons you have for stopping yourself smoking and the stronger the reasons are, the more likely it is that you will stick to your rule. You may start with just one reason – let's say you want to set a good example for your children – but if you can add others and build on these, it will strengthen your armour in the face of the spears that nicotine will throw at you.

5 **Conserve and build mental energy:** It is hard to exercise self-control when you are tired, stressed or drunk. The solution is simple: get as much sleep as you can, find ways of avoiding or dealing with stress – and don't get drunk!

Taming the horse

So if that's how to strengthen the rider, how do you tame the horse? Again there are five simple rules.

1 **Avoid triggers and create barriers:** Make your environment work in your favour, not against you. This means actively avoiding situations that are going to set off smoking urges and making it as hard as you can to get hold of cigarettes if you suffer a moment of weakness.

2 **Reduce the harmful desires/urges:** Since in the case of smoking these are coming largely from the effect of nicotine on the animal brain, I am going to strongly advise you to use some kind of cigarette substitute. These might be other nicotine products or medicines that you can get from the doctor. These really work – but only if you use them correctly. There are other more 'natural' ways of reducing smoking urges, such as physical activity and breathing exercises, but as with the cigarette substitutes, they will only be effective if you do them properly.

3 **Re-channel the harmful desires/urges:** Remember the three-spined stickleback and how it digs a hole when it can't decide whether to attack or flee? You can help yourself by finding your own 'displacement reaction'. I'll tell you some things that others have tried that could work for you.

4 **Extinguish the harmful habits:** A little earlier I told you that if a behaviour is not rewarded, it extinguishes – eventually. Unfortunately, it is hard to block the reward from nicotine because it happens automatically, but stop-smoking medicines do it to some degree. If you use these medicines in a particular way, you could get more out of them than you think – I will explain how.

5 **Train competing habits:** If you can find something to do instead of smoking that you find rewarding, it will help to beat the temptations to smoke. I don't know you well enough to say what will work for you, but later in the book I will discuss some possibilities.

So all the ingredients in Part Two of *The SmokeFree Formula* are going, in some way or another, to strengthen the rider that is your rational mind and tame the horse of your animal brain's desire to smoke. Not all of them will work for you, but if you follow my guidance and your own experience, you will give yourself the best chance of staying off cigarettes for good each time that you try.

Addiction

You may have noticed that I haven't really talked about addiction yet. That is because I wanted you to understand what is driving your smoking without using this label. But now I can tell you what scientists mean by 'addiction' and how nicotine makes cigarettes addictive when nicotine skin patches are not.

The first thing to realise is that addiction doesn't make you *do* things – it makes you *want, need* or *feel the urge* to do them. So addictions don't control your behaviour – they control *you* …

Everything I have talked about in Chapter 2 when it comes to behaviour applies equally to addiction. I hope you can see that there is nothing particularly special about these behaviours that we call 'addictions'. They are subject to the same influences as any other behaviour – it is just that the motivational forces driving them are stronger, and the consequences can be very bad.

What is nicotine addiction?

A lot of people think of addiction as a physical dependence on a drug – that people need to keep their body topped up with the drug to prevent dangerous or nasty withdrawal symptoms. So the alcoholic needs to drink to prevent epileptic fits; the heroin addict needs to keep injecting to stop stomach cramps and flu-like symptoms.

The tobacco industry and nicotine addiction

There is a slightly chilling video clip on the Internet showing the seven chief executive officers of America's largest tobacco companies swearing on oath before Congress that they believed that cigarettes were not addictive in 1994.

And all the time they had secret documents which showed very clearly they knew full well that nicotine in cigarettes was addictive and that their companies were engineering their products to make them as addictive as possible. They were caught out and had to pay billions in compensation to US states.

You may wonder why the NHS has not similarly received compensation from tobacco companies for the costs of smoking-related disease. I can't give you a sensible answer. It is a weakness of our legal system that – despite everyone knowing that cigarettes are addictive and lethal – we cannot successfully sue the manufacturers for promoting them and pretending for decades that they aren't.

However almost no one in the scientific community thinks of addiction like that any more. This is for a very good reason: if that were all there was to addiction it would be very easy to cure it. All we would need to do would be to take addicts into hospital, give them drugs to help with the withdrawal symptoms and gradually wean them off. They would emerge a month or two later 'cured'. And, in the case of stimulant drugs such as cocaine, there aren't even particularly strong withdrawal symptoms.

In fact it is relatively easy to 'detox' if you are addicted to cigarettes. You book yourself into a health farm and don't touch a cigarette for a month. The problem is that when you come out you would still experience those strong urges to smoke that I referred to earlier. The real issue comes from dealing with the powerful urges to go back to the addictive drug afterwards. This tells us that withdrawal symptoms are only part of the story of addiction.

So addiction has to be defined in a way that reflects the real problem – and the real problem is that we have people finding themselves doing something they truly wish they weren't doing, but when they try to control their use, they can't.

And of course I have explained that this is because the animal part of our brains generates powerful wants and needs, which the human part of our brain struggles to control. Particular drugs and some behaviours have the power to tap into that animal part of our brain directly. Each drug of addiction acts in different ways, but in the end that is what it boils down to.

What this means is that to stop being addicted, we need to subdue the animal part of our brain and give extra strength to the human part. To use the metaphor I talked about when describing the psychology of behaviour, we need to 'strengthen the rider and tame the horse'. That is what everything in this book seeks to do for you.

Why isn't everyone addicted to cigarettes?

Cigarettes are addictive because the nicotine in cigarettes gives you powerful urges to smoke. For most people, smoking creates a cross between an itch that needs scratching, a hunger that needs satisfying and a thirst that needs quenching. But this is not the case for everyone.

We have all heard about people who smoked 40 cigarettes a day but then just stopped – no problem! Many of these stories will have been embellished – but it does happen. Our bodies and brains are all different. Not everyone who smokes gets lung cancer. Not everyone who smokes becomes addicted. Or rather, addiction is not all or nothing – it is a matter of degree.

In this sense, being addicted is a bit like being overweight: we can all recognise the extremes, but it's easy to kid yourself that your problem is less serious than it really is.

How addicted are you?

With weight, we can at least take a long, hard look in the mirror, or at the scales. But how do you know how addicted you are?

Quite a good measure is when you have to light up your first cigarette of the day. If you can't last more than a few minutes, that is a good sign. Addiction to cigarettes involves strong urges to smoke when you find yourself in situations where you would normally light up. So even if you don't experience these urges every day, another useful test of addiction is just how strong your urges to smoke are when you do experience them.

Addiction-level questionnaire

Here are two of the most important questions to ask yourself to discover how addicted you are. (You have already seen the second one – it was used to measure your urges to smoke.)

1. When do you usually light up your first cigarette of the day?

• Within five minutes of waking	(score 3)
• Between five and thirty minutes of waking	(score 2)
• Between thirty minutes and an hour after waking	(score 1)
• More than an hour after waking	(score 0)

2. When you experience urges to smoke, how strong are they?

• I don't experience any urges	(score 0)
• Slight urges	(score 1)
• Moderate urges	(score 2)
• Strong urges	(score 3)
• Very strong urges	(score 4)
• Extremely strong urges	(score 5)

Add up your two numbers to get a score out of eight, then use the chart below to see how you compare with other smokers. This will give you some idea of how difficult you are likely to find it to stop, based on our research with nearly 40,000 smokers.

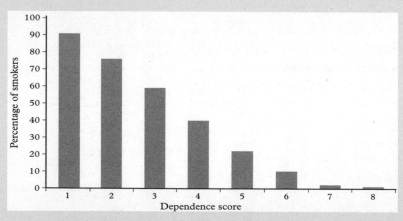

Fig 3.1 Smokers' addiction levels

So 90 per cent of smokers have a score of one or more, 75 per cent have a score of two or more, 60 per cent have a score of three or more, 40 per cent have a score of four or more ... Now we start to get to the more dependent smokers: 20 per cent have a score of five or more, 10 per cent have a score of 6 or more, and if you score 7 or 8, you are in the top 2 per cent of dependence.

Apart from the strength of your urges to smoke and the time from waking to your first cigarette of the day, there are a few other things that will tell you how difficult you could find staying off cigarettes. One of these is how long you have managed to stay off cigarettes in the past. If you have managed to stay off for several months or years before, then you stand a better chance of managing it this time. That is not too surprising – one of the most important lessons in psychology is that our past behaviour usually predicts our future behaviour.

Another one, which won't surprise you, is whether you have a partner who smokes – and, to a lesser extent, friends who smoke. This is something that has to be tackled head on, and *The Smoke-Free Formula* will provide some ingredients to do this.

As I mentioned earlier, the older you are, the more likely you are to succeed long-term in stopping if you try, though you are less likely to try. There is nothing you can do about your age, but knowing something about why these trends exist could help you boost your chances of success.

Just like intelligence and many other characteristics, a large chunk of your degree of addiction to cigarettes is down to your own particular genetic make-up. For cigarettes, about half of the difference between people's levels of addiction is the result of genetic variations. This is pretty similar to dependence on other drugs. This means that if your father or mother were smokers who had difficulty stopping, there is a fair chance that you will as well. It's not inevitable – it's just a probability.

We also know something about what genes are involved. Some of them are genes to do with the chemical dopamine that I told you about earlier; some of them are to do with the brain receptors for the chemical acetylcholine (which nicotine imitates); and some are to do with how quickly your liver is able to get rid of nicotine from your body.

The reason I'm telling you this is that it reinforces the point that none of this is your fault (if it's anyone's fault, it's the tobacco companies that know how to make money from your animal brain) – *but you can do something about it.*

Chapter 4

Why do you Want to Stop Smoking?

I've talked a lot about how nicotine keeps you smoking. Now let's look at the other side of the coin. To give your 'rider' (or rational mind) strength, it's a good idea to be very clear about why you are stopping because you will need to remind yourself of those reasons if the going gets tough.

I explained in Chapter 2 how our rational beliefs have to be united with our animal desires to make us do things. Well, having your reasons for stopping fresh in your head can help do that. I'll go through the main five here to help you get that clear picture in mind.

1. Being healthy

Do you get out of breath easily? Do you have a smokers' cough? Do you already have heart trouble? Do you have back pain? Do you suffer from anxiety or depression? These are all conditions that smoking causes or makes worse. The Benefits of Quitting Smoking in the appendix gives you a full list. Some of these may surprise you.

I'm not saying this to make you feel bad or frighten you. I just want to make sure you know all the facts. If you are already suffering from one of these conditions, stopping smoking can make a huge difference to whether it gets worse or better.

Roll-up cigarettes

Nowadays about 30 per cent of smokers smoke hand-rolled cigarettes, and the main reason for this is that they are cheaper. Some smokers think they are safer because they don't have the same additives. Sadly, they are not really safer – it is the tobacco that is the main harmful ingredient.

I looked into whether smokers are less likely to try to stop or to succeed in stopping if they smoke cheap cigarettes or roll-ups. You might imagine that this would make a difference because cost might be less of an issue. However, the research says it makes no difference at all.

There is one thing in particular I want to mention. It's a disease called COPD – chronic obstructive pulmonary disease. About one in ten smokers over 40 years of age suffers from it, mostly in a mild form. Most of these do not know it. But if you tend to cough in the mornings or at night, or if you find that colds go to your chest and last a long time, it would be worth getting yourself checked out. What happens is that the lining of your lungs and airways become inflamed, your lungs lose their elasticity, the little pockets called alveoli break down and the airways become blocked.

The reason I particularly want to single out COPD is that it is a progressive disease so you want to stop it as early as possible – and the only way of doing that is to stop smoking. You certainly don't want to wait until it gets so bad that you are out of breath from just walking. The way to get it checked is simply to book an appointment with your doctor and say that you would like your lungs checked. Feel free to say that Professor West suggested it!

Whatever happens, it will be worth it. If you are given the all-clear that will give you a good reason to stop smoking so that you can stay that way. If your doctor tells you that you have the beginnings of COPD, then you have even more reason to stop smoking right away.

Anyway, if health is an important reason for stopping, that is great. We have found that smokers who stop for health reasons are more likely to succeed long-term.

2. Saving money

The average smoker in Britain spends about £26 each week on cigarettes. You probably have quite a good idea how much you spend. A lot of this goes to the government. But you would probably rather have this money yourself. If cigarettes were incredibly enjoyable, you might think the eye-watering cost is worth it – but, as you know yourself, they mostly aren't.

In Chapter 12 I'll tell you about different ways in which you can count the savings you are making by not smoking. For now, I just want to acknowledge that cost is a very sensible reason for wanting to stop and tell you that our research shows that smokers who are stopping for this reason are more likely to succeed long-term.

3. You've just 'had enough'

If you can't imagine it, you can't want it. That is one of the important lessons I'm trying to teach you about the psychology of smoking. Imagining being a non-smoker could be a very good starting point for successfully quitting.

A lot of smokers know the feeling: the romance of smoking has worn off. Everything that attracted you to cigarettes in the first place – wanting to look cool, acting like a grown up, trying to relieve stress – now appears to be an illusion. Instead of lighting up and feeling like a Hollywood movie star, you find yourself out in the rain, huddled underneath a friend's umbrella, coughing between unsatisfying puffs on a cigarette. You don't have enough money for the things you really want, but somehow you find yourself buying yet another pack of cigarettes to feed an unhealthy addiction. It doesn't make any sense, and it's time to change.

This is the feeling that you have 'had enough'. It's a common one: only about 20 per cent of smokers like being a smoker, and most are driven by habit or addiction. The visceral feeling that you just don't want to do it anymore is a common trigger for stopping and it may be one that works for you.

If this sounds like you – do remember it. The feeling can set you off on just the right track. It's not essential, but it might be helpful. If things get tough, you can come back to the sense that you've just 'had enough'.

4. Breaking free from addiction

We sometimes joke about being addicted to things like coffee and chocolate. In fact when I used to lecture at Royal Holloway London University, I did a survey of what things the students thought they were addicted to. Horse riding and shopping came high on the list! (I think that might say something about the kinds of students who used to go to that college …)

But liking doing something a lot, and even liking it although it is naughty and we shouldn't do it, doesn't really count as addiction. We do lots of things that we like and which are a little bad for us. I hope I've been able to convince you in the previous chapter that addiction is not that at all.

Create a message for your future self

Right now you really want to stop for one or more of the reasons I have talked about. But the mind is very fickle – and nicotine plays tricks on you to try to get you to forget why you are not smoking.

If you have a smartphone with a video camera, or any other kind of webcam or video recorder, try just turning it on and sending a message to yourself in the future telling yourself why you are stopping and how important it is to you. Actually there is a smartphone app designed exactly for that purpose – it's called 'memo2self'.

All you have to do is to make a promise to yourself that, if you are tempted to have a cigarette, you will wait until you have played that message back to yourself.

It's like time travel. Your past self is reminding your future self of something it has forgotten.

Of course you could always write it down on a piece of paper, or record a message to yourself on a recording device and that could work as well. But a video is much more immediate, and so I think it might be even better.

I don't know for sure if this will help you quit, but I think it's definitely worth a shot.

We interviewed a wide range of people who had stopped smoking to ask about their experiences so you can see what ingredients other people have succeeded with. These stories will appear throughout the book. This is the first of them.

Keith – 52 years old – *stopped after a health scare*
Keith took early retirement for health reasons. He previously worked in the health sector.

I started smoking when I was round about nine or ten years old. I started because of peer pressure. I think my sister came round with a friend and they were smoking. They gave me a cigarette and I just took a lug. And that was it: I was hooked. Smoking was very much advertised and pushed as a hip thing. It was advertised on the TV; it looked good to smoke; it made you feel grown up about yourself. Psychologically, you felt like an adult. That was part of society in those days. It was cheap.

This is a common story – tobacco companies pushing their products, youngsters aspiring to be grown up, low cost, peer pressure, rapidly becoming addicted ...

I didn't see smoking as a problem at first and didn't think about stopping. I think when I started trying to stop I was in my early to mid twenties. I was unsuccessful. The longest I got was about two or three days.

Young people typically try to stop more often but they also have greatest difficulty making it stick.

Then I tried using different stop-smoking products. I think the first thing on the market was nicotine chewing gum. That didn't work for me. The first tablet they brought out – they called it a miracle tablet – was Zyban. That didn't work either. Then I tried Champix and that didn't work. I've used every single option there was to stop smoking.

My guess is that, as a heavily addicted smoker, Keith would have needed more than the standard dose of these medicines.

Back then, people could smoke in pubs, you could smoke on the bus, you could smoke on trains – I think trying to stop smoking was a very difficult thing to do for any individual, because it was there everywhere you went. If you went to the pictures, you could sit and smoke. Ashtrays used to be on the back of chairs.

When the smoking ban came in, it made it easier for smokers to stop.

.

Then I started seeing what sort of smoker I was. I wasn't smoking for the enjoyment of smoking, I was smoking for the nicotine. It was an addiction – quite a bad one. My smoking got worse as time went on. I was smoking something like 60–70 fags a day.

The peak age for nicotine addiction seems to be around 40.

Then something went 'bang'. I had a brain aneurysm that left me blind in one eye and partially sighted in the other. Since that day, 9 February 2009, I've never had another cigarette.

Sometimes it takes an incident like this to break the hold that cigarettes have over you.

The damage has been done, I know that. But it's been four years since I smoked a cigarette. And I'm very proud of it. I don't get chesty as I did. I don't get the coughing and shortness of breath.

Keith may not have escaped scot-free, but by stopping relatively young he has avoided a lot of other health problems.

I now look back on my time as a smoker with deep regret – for many different reasons. Most of all, health. Secondly, financial reasons: I'd be a very rich man; I'd have bought my house a couple of times over.

Keith definitely identifies himself as a non-smoker (Ingredient 2) – he certainly doesn't look back on smoking with any kind of fondness.

> The biggest lesson I learned was this: you pay to kill yourself. How extraordinary is that? Because smoking kills. I used to wake up in the middle of the night for a fag. But I wasn't waking up for the fag, I was waking up for the nicotine.
>
> *Keith beautifully expresses the strange hold that cigarettes can take on your life.*

Addiction is when what you are doing is causing real harm and you don't particularly like it, but it has got a hold over you so that you are trapped. It is a form of servitude, a bondage to your animal brain. None of us likes to feel that we are a slave, but that is what addiction feels like. Whatever other reasons you might have for stopping smoking, breaking free from addiction to cigarettes is definitely one to have on your list.

And the longer you are able to stay off cigarettes, the closer to freedom you become. That makes the goal of liberation a very useful tool to keep with you throughout your journey. Even months after you have stopped, when you are thinking that you might have just one cigarette, *remember the hold that cigarettes had over you – you really don't want that to happen again.*

5. For your family

The last common reason for stopping I will talk about is for the sake of the family. This can take many different forms. In my case it was my girlfriend, later to become my wife, who didn't like my smoking. And, when I think about it, it wasn't nice for her to have to kiss me smelling of cigarettes. Frankly, I'm surprised she did it! So your partner might be one factor in your decision to stop.

Quite a lot of smokers want to stop for the sake of their children or grandchildren. Obama famously said he stopped in the end because he wanted to be able to look his daughters in the eye and say he did not smoke.

I hear a lot of smokers saying that they want to stop to set a good example for their children. And they are probably spot on. There are studies showing that if one or both of a teenager's parents stop smoking, they are less likely to take it up themselves. We often think that teenagers don't take any notice of their parents, but when it comes to things like this, it seems that they do. Perhaps this is a reassuring message – if we can stop, that is.

Of course there are many more people in our families than our children and partners. Perhaps you have special people you are quitting for. Whoever it is, it is a very good reason for quitting, and it is very helpful to remember this reason when things start to get difficult.

So those are the main reasons that smokers give for stopping. A lot of smokers have more than one reason, and that is a very good thing – my research shows that *the more reasons you have, the more likely you are to stay off cigarettes when you try*. So do keep thinking about them.

Chapter 5

Ways to Quit

We are getting close now to the point where you will get going with your quit attempt, if you haven't already.

Deciding when and how you are going to stop can make a difference to how long you last and even whether you succeed permanently. There is a lot to consider, so let's have a look at the options.

Stop right away

About half of quit attempts are made the moment the smoker has decided to quit. You might think that these impulsive attempts would not last so long, but you'd be wrong – they last at least as long as ones where the smoker makes plans by setting a quit date for some point in the future. So if you feel ready to stop right now, then it is perfectly fine to do that.

An important message of *The SmokeFree Formula* is: if you feel you want to stop right now, then do it.

But there are other options, which are totally fine, if you want to prepare the ground.

r e s e a r c h

To plan or not to plan – that is the question

Some people will tell you that you must plan your quit attempt in advance to have a good chance of success. That is not true.

Some years ago a diminutive figure appeared in my office doorway in Bloomsbury. It was a Canadian GP who wanted to talk to me about a paper that she had submitted to the scientific journal, *Addiction* (<http://www.addictionjournal.org>), of which I am the editor-in-chief. The paper had been rejected out of hand.

Her name was Lynn Larabie and she had done a study in which she had interviewed 100 or so patients about their smoking and how they gave up. She had found that about half of those who had tried to stop had started the attempt the moment they had made the decision – they had not planned it in advance, not even for later that day.

This was surprising because the received wisdom was that people had to progress through a series of stages before they tried to quit.

What was more surprising was that the smokers who had tried to stop the moment they made the decision were *more likely* still not to be smoking at the time when Dr Larabie spoke to them than those who planned their quit in advance. So it seemed that planning the quit attempt was not such a good idea.

Dr Larabie's paper had been rejected by one of my editors. I thought that this was because it was not particularly well presented and, although the message was interesting and novel, it needed a lot of work to get it into shape. So I set about helping Dr Larabie to get it into shape, and after a few weeks we were ready to send it back to my own journal – its shape was perfect! And it was promptly rejected again.

Anyone who thinks that getting scientific work published is a rational, logical process had better think again. It is done by humans – and we humans are full of prejudices and errors. Anyway, we sent it to a rival journal whose editor immediately saw that it was an important study and it ended up being published. I then did essentially the same study on a much larger sample, got the same result and it was published in one of the world's top medical journals.

The newspaper headlines that followed unfortunately missed the point – they thought the study showed that it was a bad thing to plan quitting in advance. But it didn't. It showed that people who had got to the point where they didn't want to wait a second longer before quitting did better than those who wanted to put it off for a bit – which isn't the same thing at all. So much depends upon you: do you really want to stop or only feel that you should want to?

Smoking triggers

One way to think about the process of quitting is in terms of feeling what I call 'tension' and 'triggers'.

By 'tension' I mean having a feeling of discomfort with the current situation but not enough to make you do anything about it right now. That is true for so many things, from having a full bladder at night or having worrying pains in your chest to being unhappy in a relationship or being concerned about smoking.

Then along comes a 'trigger' – a stimulus that turns the discomfort into action. It could be something as simple as the fact that the discomfort gets too much, or someone says something, or you see someone else doing the act. Triggers can be large or small – sometimes you don't even notice them – an idea just pops into your head and you act.

So when you suddenly decide: that's it, no more smoking – it could be something big or small that is the final trigger, but usually there will have been tensions niggling away in the background.

Set a quit date in the next couple of weeks

Sometimes it makes perfect sense to set your quit date for some point in the future. If you are going to use one of the stop-smoking medicines or see a professional stop-smoking advisor, you will need to plan that in advance.

The only thing I would say is: don't leave it too long and be very clear about what the date is going to be. The longer you leave it, the more likely it is that you will go off the idea and your chance will have slipped away.

I think that if you are going to delay quitting a little, it should be for a very good reason and you should start out with a clear idea that you have made the commitment to try.

Choosing a special date to stop

It is quite common for smokers to tie in a quit attempt with a special date. It might be New Year, No Smoking Day, a birthday or an anniversary. I don't know, but I think that this might help, simply by making the date a bit more memorable. What you are trying to do is to create as clean a break as possible between you as a smoker and you as a non-smoker, and this might help.

Buying cars and stopping smoking

If you have ever bought a car from a showroom or used-car lot, you will know that once the salesperson has got you in his or her sights, he or she will do everything possible to close a deal before you set foot off the premises.

Car salesmen know from experience that if you leave without signing on the dotted line, they have probably lost you: *even if you yourself strongly believe that you will be back later to sign.*

It's the same with stopping smoking. We go on and off the boil. One minute you can be thinking, 'That's it. I've had enough of this – I'm going to stop.' But if you don't act on it, one week later this is a distant memory. The moment has passed.

My friend and colleague Professor John Hughes is a psychiatrist in Vermont, USA. We were among the first researchers to show that the symptoms smokers experienced when they tried to stop were due to nicotine withdrawal. Professor Hughes did a very neat study which I think shows just how important it is to stop when the moment strikes and not to delay longer than is necessary.

He took a group of volunteer smokers who were interested in quitting. Half of them were advised to set a quit date within the next one to three weeks, and half were advised to cut down gradually and set a quit date for three to five weeks' time. Perhaps you won't be surprised to learn that those who were advised to set their quit date later were less likely even to make a quit attempt. Yet these two groups had started out exactly the same.

I can't be totally certain, but I think it was the advice to delay quitting that led to these smokers' failure to quit.

We like anniversaries. They are things to look forward to and also look back on. My birthday is in June and I remember being glad about that because, with Christmas in December, I never had to wait more than six months for the next lot of presents!

I can't tell you that your quit attempt will last longer if you save it up for an anniversary, but I do know that a lot of people find anniversaries and special occasions to be a useful spur to action. And I think that linking a quit attempt to a special day can give it that little bit of extra impetus.

New Year is the biggest time of year for quitting in a lot of countries, with the tradition of the 'New Year's resolution'. In Britain about half a million smokers try to stop around New Year.

In the UK there is also the institution of 'No Smoking Day' on the second Wednesday of March each year. There is usually quite a bit of publicity around it. Certainly No Smoking Day acts as a spur to quitting – around 300,000 more smokers try to stop than would otherwise give it a go. And in 2012 a new event was launched in England called 'Stoptober'. The idea was for smokers to commit to not smoking for the whole month and to turn this into a mass movement. Many more people quit that October than usual, so the early signs are very promising.

Choosing the time of day

You're going to have to choose a time of day to make the break. There is something to be said for making it first thing in the morning because it is the start of a new day and a chapter in your life. For many smokers, the desire for a cigarette is often lower first thing in the morning and builds up over the day. So you might find it a bit easier to get started then …

On the other hand, there is a lot to be said for smoking normally until the early evening and then packing it in. The reason is that urges to smoke tend to be higher at that time of day and, if you can get over the first evening while you are still very fresh, it may be easier.

There isn't any evidence one way or the other, but I recommend that you make a *definite decision* and stick to it.

Choosing the day of the week

It seems perfectly reasonable to ask what day of the week gives you the best chance of success when you stop. Is it a weekday – perhaps Monday? Or is it Saturday or Sunday? When I ask friends and colleagues what they think, I get a variety of answers – all of which are very sensible.

Well, as it happens I have recently looked at this and found that success for the first four weeks at least is similar for all the days except for one – which is about 70 per cent higher. And that day is Sunday.

I need to confirm this with further studies but if you are thinking about quitting on a particular day you might want to bear that in mind.

Choosing the right conditions

It can be hard to do anything difficult when you are under stress. Exercising self-control requires mental energy and this will be lower when you have other things going on in your life. There aren't any studies that can tell you whether this would be the right approach for you, but if you aren't ready to stop for whatever reason, it makes sense to leave it until you are. When you get going, you want everything to be working in your favour.

Or you can quit anyway and not wait till you are stress-free. Although it makes sense to wait until everything is running smoothly in your life before trying to stop, we have some research which found that if people stopped even when they were under stress, they did just as well as those who stopped when everything was fine. Again, this could be because that feeling of really wanting to stop is so important. So if you are ready to go, then I suggest you don't delay – strike while the iron is hot.

The 'Not a puff' rule

So what does all this add up to? I would like to be able to tell you exactly when to stop to give yourself the best chance, but I don't have the evidence to do that. In any event it may be one of those things that is very different for different people.

All I would say is, whatever you do, make it a deliberate choice: from this point on, no more cigarettes. The rule I tell people is: **not a puff**! Because a single puff can very easily lead to another puff, and, before you know it, you're back to being a smoker again. Choose your cut-off point and stick to it.

Part Two

The Ingredients

Your SmokeFree Formula

When you're trying to give up smoking it's important to know your enemy. That's why I've spent quite a long time telling you about smoking, why you smoke and why you have found it hard to stop. All this information will help you understand why some of the ingredients you are going to learn about could really work for you.

In Part One I explained how *The SmokeFree Formula* works: the secret of stopping is to keep trying and every time you try to create your own formula that will give you the best chance of lasting success. Now it's time for you to get involved.

I'm assuming that you have made a clear decision to stop smoking – either now or in the very near future. Part Two is all about helping you choose the best way to try to quit.

Think of this section as a storehouse full of useful ingredients sitting on shelves waiting for you to use them. Everything in here is something I think might help you stop smoking. Each chapter groups together a collection of ingredients that I think will help you in a different way. So you should at least have a think about whether you want to use something from each chapter, so as to build as many defences as possible against the temptations of nicotine.

I'm going to explain how each ingredient works and show you how to pick ones that will help achieve your goal of getting cigarettes out of your life for good.

An ingredient is anything that could help you stop smoking.

Each chapter may have up to half a dozen ingredients. You can select as many as you like from each chapter – and from the book as a whole. I will tell you about the best available scientific evidence, but it is up to you to take control and decide what you want to do. Remember, the principle of *The SmokeFree Formula* is: I guide – you decide.

Each ingredient will get a star rating, which is based on the best available evidence and tells you whether I think it is likely to be helpful. Here are the ratings and what they mean:

★★★   I think there is strong evidence this can help you stay off cigarettes.
★★   I have reason to think this will help but I don't have good evidence.
★   I really can't say whether this will make a difference for you, but it might.

It's important to say what these ratings are *not*. Ingredients with three stars are not automatically the best, and it may not be right for you to build a formula of just everything with a three-star rating. What the stars tell you is how confident I am that an ingredient will be of *some* use to you.

Three stars mean we know something works *on average*. But everyone is different. Even if some of the other ingredients aren't as tried and tested, they could work for you. I have put nothing in here which I think is useless. I'll tell you what I think the most important ingredients are, but you must use your own judgement to choose what you think will work.

Your job is to make a note of each ingredient you might want to use. Chapter 15 will then help you put these ingredients together to make your own formula.

A formula is a collection of your chosen ingredients.

Some ingredients are more important than others. Personally, I think the most important questions to think about are:

• Will you see a trained stop-smoking advisor if there is one available to you?

- Will you use one of the nicotine products or stop-smoking medicines, and if so, which one?
- Will you stop abruptly or cut down gradually?
- Will you decide to take on a new identity in which smoking plays no part?

The SmokeFree Formula website

Now is a good time to introduce you to the website that accompanies this book: <http://www.smokefreeformula.com>. It is totally free. There are lots of stop-smoking websites out there and I will talk about them a little later. This one is different and is especially for you.

The SmokeFree Formula website does three things:

1 It shows you an up-to-the minute chart of how successful each ingredient is proving for all the smokers who register on the website and report what they are using and how they have got on. This could be invaluable when making your own choice.
2 It allows you to exchange information with other users on how exactly you are using each ingredient and what you think are the upsides and downsides. This is through a kind of Twitter feed.
3 It provides links to the most up-to-date scientific research on each of the ingredients – this is very important because we get new information in all the time.

Do please register – it will grow and become more helpful the more it is used.

You might be thinking: 'How can I possibly pick from dozens of ingredients?' Well, in addition to the star ratings and your own experience, I have put together a guide below to get you on your way. Some of what I am suggesting is obvious but I think it is worth highlighting anyway.

Make a note of the ingredients that it suggests for you, but remember – these are only suggestions.

The ingredients that are not mentioned in this table – 21, 22, 23, 25, 27, 28 – should be ones that anyone could benefit from.

Quick guide to choosing your ingredients

All about you	Have a close look at these ingredients
If you feel comfortable about stopping cigarettes without cutting down first	1
If you have had enough of being a 'smoker'	2
If you prefer not to look too far ahead	3
If you are happy to talk to a health professional about your smoking, and can set aside some time each week to talk to someone	4, 5
If you feel comfortable using computers or phones to get information	6, 7, 9
If you like reading or there is a particular book that grabs you (apart from this one)	8
If you smoke ten or more cigarettes per day, you smoke soon after waking up or you experience quite strong urges to smoke	10, 11, 12, 13, 14
If you have hobbies or things that you particularly like doing	15
If you are happy to share the fact that you are stopping with other people	16, 18
If you are fed up with the amount of money you are spending on cigarettes	17
If you have someone who would make a good quitting companion	18
If you have particular situations where you usually light up	19
If it is realistic for you to be able to stay away from other smokers for a while, at least in social situations	20
If you enjoy exercising (which includes going for walks)	24
If you are worried about putting on weight	24, 26, 29

Where my evidence comes from

I have promised that everything in this book is based on the best scientific evidence. But you might be thinking: 'You may be a professor, but how do I know what you're telling me is true?' It's a fair question, so in this section I'll explain how I arrived at my conclusions.

You don't have to read this bit; it's not essential to stopping, and if you want, you can skip ahead to the next chapter to get cracking on the ingredients. But, speaking personally, I would like you to have a stab at reading this because understanding what the evidence means will make it easier to decide which ingredients might work for you. What's more, how we approach truth and evidence is important in so much of our lives that I think it could help you with everything from buying a new fridge to electing a politician.

Scientific Truth

Science is about shaping our beliefs so that they are closer to the truth. Contrary to what a lot of people think, it is not usually about being certain. When new evidence comes along, we change our minds and get a bit nearer to reality. There are not too many cast-iron guarantees in this process, but there are a lot of strong probabilities.

Take the science of weather forecasting. We complain about weather forecasts and of course forecasters cannot predict for sure whether it will rain on your street in 24 hours' time. But they can give you a good idea of your *chances* of getting wet. You can use that information to decide whether or not to carry an umbrella, wear a raincoat or stay at home. And, actually, weather forecasting has got a lot more accurate in recent decades – it estimates those chances pretty well.

The science of stopping smoking is similar. It cannot tell you what will definitely work. But it can tell you what the chances are so that you can decide what you want to try.

No one study 'proves' anything. But the more studies we have that point in the same direction, the more confident we can be.

My star ratings for the ingredients are based on the best available evidence on how effective they are likely to be. There are some things I will talk about along the way that won't get into my list of ingredients. This is because they haven't been tested, or they might help but I have important reservations about them.

What counts as evidence?

In medical science there are methods for finding things out and, while these can never provide absolute certainty, they provide varying levels of confidence.

Let's take the example of hypnotherapy. There are literally thousands of hypnotherapists advertising on the Internet – telling you that their method will help you to stop smoking. In fact my Google search for the phrase 'hypnotherapy to help you stop smoking' brings up almost 6 million hits. Some of them claim success rates of 90 per cent or they say that success is 'guaranteed'.

How do they know? The answer is of course that they don't. They are saying that to get you to buy what they are selling. They may passionately believe that their method is the greatest thing since sliced bread, but there is very little evidence to back them up.

So how do we learn about the effectiveness of a particular stop-smoking method?

Randomised Control Trials (RCTs)

The RCT was recently selected by several leading experts as the greatest medical advance of the twentieth century – ahead even of vaccines and antibiotics. That's because the RCT is one of the basic building blocks of medicine, a tool for finding out whether something truly works.

Imagine someone develops a pill they claim could cure the common cold. They get hundreds of people with colds to take the pill – and a month later almost all of them are better. A miracle cure? Well, no. As everyone knows, most colds go away in a month – pill or no pill. To say the cold went away because of the pill would be like watching people eat ice cream on a sunny day and concluding that, because one happens after the other, eating ice cream causes sunburn.

Snake oil and washing machines

There is a long tradition of unscrupulous or misguided entrepreneurs selling fake or even dangerous 'cures' or 'quack remedies'. The history of medicine is littered with this kind of practice. Doctors used to cut patients and put leeches on their skin to let their blood out in the belief that it would cure a range of illnesses. In the Wild West in the United States medicine men would famously go from town to town selling 'snake oil' as a cure for all known ills.

Nowadays we have government regulation to try to prevent this happening. If you want to claim that a drug or device has some curative properties you have to put it through a series of tests of the kind I am going to describe and you are strictly limited about what you can say. That makes very good sense: just as I cannot advertise and sell washing machines that don't work or will electrocute you when you turn them on.

But we have no such protection against people making bogus claims for their 'cure' for smoking. Yet stopping smoking is at least as important as having a working washing machine – it may not give clean clothes but it does give life and health.

So you have to rely on your common sense and advice from people like me. And my first piece of advice is: if someone offers a *guaranteed* cure for smoking, don't touch it with a barge pole. The only thing they can guarantee is that they will take your money off you.

The only way to test whether a pill or any other medicine works is to compare two groups of people who you believe are the same in every way – except for the intervention you want to test.

So in an RCT, we take a fairly large number of people (say 500) and ask them to take part in an experiment. In that experiment, we decide at 'random' (using what is in effect the toss of a coin) whether they get treatment 'X' or something that we don't think is going to work so well – what we call a 'control condition'. We then look to see what happens.

If X is worthwhile, more people should be cured when given that treatment than in the control condition. The more people we include in our RCT and the bigger the difference in the outcome between X and the control group, the more confident we can be in the result.

There are well-established statistical methods for working out this degree of confidence, and by convention we expect to see at least two independent studies each showing a benefit for X that we are more than 95 per cent sure is not down to chance before we say – yes, X probably works.

Let's go back to hypnotherapy. Has it been tested in this rigorous way to see if it helps with stopping smoking? Well, yes, to some degree. There are 11 rather small RCTs in the scientific literature.

The research shows us that hypnotherapy is probably better than just brief advice: 48 out of 202 people given hypnotherapy (24 per cent) were not smoking six months after the treatment, compared with only 29 out of 194 (15 per cent) who just got brief advice. That means that nine people out of every hundred who tried hypnotherapy stopped smoking for at least six months who would not have done if they had just got brief advice. It's not a massive number, but it is worthwhile.

When hypnotherapy was compared with a more extended conversation with someone about stopping smoking, the advantage narrowed: 41 out of 246 people (17 per cent) were not smoking after hypnotherapy compared with 33 out of 246 (13 per cent) who talked to an advisor. So really there does not seem to be anything special about hypnotherapy that you wouldn't get with talking to someone who just gave you some practical advice.

So what can we say about hypnotherapy? I think there is enough evidence to say that it *might* help, but it has not been tested on enough people for me to be very confident, and I don't see any good evidence that it works better than simple practical advice.

I will apply the same scrutiny to all the ingredients I mention in this book. Some will do better than hypnotherapy and some will do worse.

And if you have tried hypnotherapy and found it helpful in the past, then please remember, my motto in *The SmokeFree Formula* is 'I guide – you decide'. You're in charge of your quit attempt – not me.

Other kinds of evidence

Good as RCTs are, they can't tell the whole story – because what happens in an experiment does not always reflect what happens in real life when the scientists have gone home. And sometimes you just can't do an RCT, either for ethical or practical reasons. So I won't just use evidence from RCTs to advise you. We need other pieces of information as well.

Here is a case in point. There are more than 100 RCTs which together lead most of us in the scientific community to believe that nicotine-replacement therapy, such as skin patches, gums, inhalers and lozenges, increase the chances of permanent success at stopping by about 60 per cent.

So you might think: simple then, and rush out to your nearest pharmacy! But wait: evidence is emerging that when smokers just buy these products from a shop and do not seek professional support and advice, they may not help at all.

How can this be? Well, there are lots of possible reasons. One is that in the RCTs, the smokers were highly motivated to use the products properly and paid careful attention to the instructions they were given by experienced professionals. The researchers would have explained that the products are not a magic cure and just take the edge off the cravings, so the quitters also need a lot of determination. But this isn't typically what happens in real life. Smokers buying the products off the shelf don't get this advice, and they appear not to be using them properly or they are coming to them with the wrong attitude.

So, apart from RCTs, what does count as evidence in my book?

Mainly, the evidence is from taking a large group of smokers who have decided of their own accord to try one or other method of stopping, then comparing how they get on. So in my large surveys of smokers, I ask who has tried to stop in the past year, what they did, how long ago it was and whether they are still not smoking. I also get them to give me some information about themselves to help me tell whether those might influence the results.

In some ways this is not as good as an RCT because different types of smokers may choose different methods and I can't be absolutely sure that any difference in outcomes was not due to that rather than the method they chose. However it does tell me what happens out there in the real world, and not just what happens when people volunteer to allow me to choose what method they will use to stop.

When I don't have that kind of information, I will use experiments that tell me whether an ingredient helps prevent or subdue urges to smoke. And when I don't have that kind of information,

I will use my judgement based on what I think underpins cigarette addiction.

So my star rating includes evidence from RCTs as well as other kinds of research that shape my beliefs. Where I think the evidence is weaker, or I am relying on my own judgement, I will say so. I will try to be as objective as possible and always remember: I guide – you decide.

Now let's get started on the ingredients of your formula …

Chapter 7

Your Approach

This chapter is all about you. How are *you* going to approach your attempt to quit?

I have to be honest with you: the evidence for what I am going to tell you is not quite as strong as for some of the later ingredients. There will be a lot of advice here that is my best guess on the basis of what evidence we have been able to gather. But I think you will find what I have to say helpful.

The first thing I have to tell you is this: I don't think anything will help you stop if you come to the quit attempt with the wrong approach. If you're coming to it reluctantly, if deep down you don't really want to stop and if you don't make stopping your number one priority for the next few weeks – I'm afraid you probably won't stay the course.

If you are truly committed to breaking free from cigarettes, you have to be clear about what you are trying to do. Let me explain what that means.

As I keep saying, I think you should start with a clear, cast-iron rule: from now on, not a single puff on a cigarette.

I like to think in four-week chunks when it comes to quitting:

The first four weeks are definitely the hardest from the point of view of cravings and withdrawal symptoms. There may well be times when you are hanging on by the skin of your teeth. You will need to do everything you can to keep from having that fateful puff on a cigarette – remembering that, no matter what else happens, if you can resist having that puff, your brain will continue to recover and you *definitely will* be free. Having that puff *will* set you back.

The next four weeks are easier in terms of withdrawal symptoms and cravings, but if you are still finding it hard and your morale is sagging, things can still be very difficult. On the other hand, if you are finding it easier, then you can start to get complacent. That little voice inside your head can pipe up telling you that you've cracked it and now perhaps you should reward yourself with a cigarette.

After that, things generally get easier and the real danger is not so much incessant cravings, withdrawal symptoms and the like – it is coming to terms with being a non-smoker and all that this entails. You may well miss your cigarettes – particularly when you are stressed, bored or out with friends. It's just soooo easy to pick up a cigarette and smoke it. The only thing stopping you will be the knowledge that you don't smoke any more.

Now let's look at the first ingredient in this chapter. It is probably the most important one in this section.

Ingredient 1: Stop abruptly

Rating: ★ ★ ★

Stopping abruptly means smoking normally right up until the day you want to quit and then cutting out cigarettes altogether. This may seem a strange way of going about tackling an addiction but there is good research showing that it works best – if you feel up to it.

Two thirds of attempts to stop are made abruptly. That means the smoker made no attempt to cut down before the big day. They smoked as normal, then when the day came they committed to not smoking at all – not a puff.

This may seem quite daunting, but I can tell you that quit attempts made like this tend to do better than ones that involve trying to cut down gradually. I'm not saying that gradual reduction won't work for you – just that, on average, stopping abruptly tends to do better.

At the Maudsley Hospital clinic in London, one of the most famous stop-smoking clinics in the world, they tell smokers they can smoke their heads off right up until the time of the quit-date session, which may be at 6 p.m. So you often see a crowd of smokers outside the building puffing away. It looks a bit odd, but it seems to work very well!

There may even be an advantage of smoking more than you usually would just as you are about to stop. There have been several studies looking at what they call 'aversive smoking'. The idea is that you smoke two or three cigarettes really hard until you are feeling physically sick – take lots of puffs and take the smoke right down into the lungs. Then your last memory of smoking will be one of feeling sick. These studies found that people who did this were slightly more likely to achieve lasting success in stopping.

If not abruptly, then what ...?

The alternative to stopping abruptly is to cut down gradually. I haven't put this as a separate ingredient because if you do not choose abrupt stopping, you must be choosing stopping gradually. This involves deciding on a quit date some time in the future – perhaps two weeks away – and gradually reducing the amount you smoke until it gets down to zero by that date.

This may seem logical because it means allowing your body to get used to less and less nicotine, and allows you to take adjusting to life without cigarettes one step at a time.

As it happens, research shows that this is less likely to be successful than abrupt quitting – so if you're not sure which to go for, I'd say try the abrupt approach first. However if you really don't think you can face abrupt quitting, then cutting down gradually is certainly better than not trying at all.

The question is how best to do it. A few options have been studied.

One is to give yourself a quota for the day and reduce it day by day until you reach zero. The problem with doing it this way is that, as you get down to just a few cigarettes, it gets harder and harder to cut these out. And each one becomes more and more rewarding. And you start to experience the same unpleasant nicotine-withdrawal symptoms you would have if you'd just stopped completely. But you *can* make this work if you substitute some other nicotine product for each cigarette you cut. You can read more about those in Chapter 10. And remember, you will have to be very disciplined about it – no letting yourself have 'just one more cigarette'.

Another option is to try having your first cigarette later and later in the day. If you normally smoke as soon as you wake up, wait until your morning break. Then wait until lunch. Then only smoke in the evening. And finally stop altogether. I can't tell you whether this is likely to work for you. It might. What I can tell you is that, as with the first method, it is more likely to work if you replace your cigarettes with one of the nicotine products such as gum, inhalator, or lozenge, or if you wear a nicotine patch.

Ingredient 2: Taking 'smoker' out of your identity

Rating: ★ ★

As long as you think of yourself as a smoker you will be at risk of going back to smoking. There are many different ways of taking the label 'smoker' out of your identity. Whichever one you go for, I think it will be important in protecting you from temptation.

Becoming a 'non-smoker' or 'ex-smoker'

Imagine what it would be like if you had never smoked in your life. Would you start now? Obviously not. That is true for just about all smokers. Almost no one starts smoking after the age of 25.

In China more than 50 per cent of men smoke and less than three per cent of women. What's the difference? Smoking is just not something that women do – it is at odds with the identity of most of the women there. Are the women being denied something by not smoking? Of course not.

And what would your life be like now if you had never smoked? Would you be thinking all the time that you need a cigarette? Would you even be thinking you'd quite like a cigarette but really you mustn't because of your health? Of course not. You'd just be a

Cutting down if you are not trying to stop

What can you do to reduce the harm from smoking without stopping completely?

A lot of doctors and nurses will tell you to cut down. In the past, smoking experts such as myself have thrown up our hands in horror at this. That is because of the fear that if you cut down you will feel less pressure to stop completely and you will be likely to end up smoking your remaining cigarettes harder to compensate. So it seemed like a really bad idea.

But things are different now. We now know that if you try to cut down you are more likely to go on to try to stop later; it doesn't undermine your desire to quit. We also know that if you use a nicotine product to help you cut down, you will smoke less and will be even more likely to go on to try to quit.

So my advice to you, if you are not ready to try to stop right at the moment, is to use one of the nicotine products to help you to cut down. There are all kinds of ways you can do this. I can't tell you which one will be more effective – it probably depends on you. Here are some options:

1 Try to set aside one or two days in the week when you don't smoke at all – you just use the nicotine product; a bit like the 5:2 diet, but for smoking!
2 Allocate yourself a certain number of cigarettes per day and pace yourself so that you never go over this number; I would try for a figure that is half what you would normally smoke.
3 Look at all the situations in which you normally smoke and cut out at least two of those from your routine.
4 Whatever time of day you normally start smoking, leave it at least another four hours.

If one of these is not working for you, try a different option. Just like with stopping, cutting down should be something you keep on doing until you find something that works for you. Of course all this is just for those times when you are not trying to stop. If you feel like stopping, you should go for it.

non-smoker, like the 75 per cent of the population in Britain who don't even think about it.

That is the place you want to be. When you arrive at that place you will be very unlikely to start smoking again. Why would you?

This label of being a non-smoker is one new identity that might work for you. But there are others.

My colleague Dr Eleni Vangeli interviewed a lot of smokers who had stopped successfully for at least six months and asked them about how they saw themselves. I had a theory that unless they thought of themselves as someone who doesn't even want to smoke – smoking is something that is not part of who they are – it would always be a struggle for them to resist the temptations to go back.

Certainly she found quite a few people like that who had succeeded. But what I found fascinating was that there were also a lot of smokers who did not renounce smoking but simply put a box around it with the lid tightly shut.

They recognised that they still had fond memories of smoking and would probably go back if it were not for the damage it does to health. But there was no question in their minds that they would ever go back: they had firmly decided that smoking was something they did not do any more. To me this is an *ex-smoker* identity rather than a *non-smoker* identity.

So what do you think would work for you? Does it make sense to you to renounce smoking as a stupid, disgusting waste of money? Or can you connect better with thinking about smoking as something that was part of your past which you enjoyed, but it can't be part of your future because it is just not worth it?

Whether you think of yourself an ex-smoker or as a non-smoker, one way to think about your new identity is as a suit of armour to protect you from the urges to smoke. You can imagine yourself standing serenely, smiling, as the cravings try to break through. And each time they try to batter your defences they use up a bit of their strength. Every time they fail to penetrate your protection they get weaker and weaker …

A whole new identity

Up until now I have been talking about only changing your identity by removing smoking from it. However, some people who stop smoking go one step further and take on a whole new identity. They start exercising, eating more healthily and generally decide they will turn over a new leaf.

I don't know whether this makes a difference, but I think it might. There is some research showing that smokers who exercise more and adopt a healthier diet are more likely to have stopped smoking when followed up some time later. That's not strong evidence but at least it gives you something to go on.

The main thing is to make a conscious choice about it. Who do you want to be?

Getting there in stages

You don't have to take on your new identity all in one go. Sometimes it is something that develops in stages. I know of smokers who started out just putting a toe in the water – not greatly committed to quitting but thinking they'd try it and see how they got on. After a day or so, they were still not smoking and thought they might as well continue. And then, day by day, they became more and more committed and engaged with the whole process of quitting until they got to a point, perhaps a few weeks later, where they thought, 'You know what? I've come this far. It would be silly to go back to smoking now.' And they never smoke again.

I think this is less common than jumping in at the deep end, but you will probably have a good idea as to whether that is something that would work for you.

Ingredient 3: Take it one day at a time

Rating: ★

I don't know of any studies that have looked at whether it helps to do this, but I hear it so often, and it makes so much sense, so I think it is something you should consider. The idea is that when things get really tough and your morale is low, it is very hard to think about the rest of your life without cigarettes. Then you have to say to yourself – 'I will not smoke today – and tomorrow we'll see'.

If you have tried to stop before, you will probably know that there are times when you can't look any further ahead than today. Your resources are depleted. The craving is incessant. You feel down and close to being out for the count. That is when you might want to shorten your time horizon. Just think about today for now; you can think about tomorrow when it comes.

This has got nothing to do with taking 'smoker' out of your identity. You may not even want to think about things like that. This is much more about hanging on by your fingertips; about clinging on to the ledge for dear life; about gritting your teeth. It is about continuing to say to yourself: 'I just need to get through today and tomorrow can take care of itself'. The only thing that matters – whatever you are feeling, however down, however irritable, however much the nicotine itch needs scratching – is to *not smoke*.

Your animal brain will be sending messages up to your human brain, trying to trick it into smoking. Saying you can have just one. Just one will get you through the day and then you'll be fine. Your human brain needs to shout back down – LEAVE ME ALONE!

Chapter 8

Personal Advice and Support

Three quarters of a million smokers in Britain each year use some kind of professional advice or support to help them stop smoking. Britain is unique in having this kind of support available very widely across the country and free on the NHS. Most of it is face-to-face but there is also telephone support available. It doesn't matter whether you are young or old, sick or well, the people who run Britain's stop smoking services want you to come and see them – they are passionate about what they do and are there to help.

I'll say right up front that if you find a good stop-smoking advisor, I can't think of a more powerful ingredient to put into your formula. Now I'm not saying that every stop-smoking advisor is going to be an expert – just like in any other profession there will be a range of abilities. But if you do go to see a stop-smoking advisor, I'll show you what he or she should be doing to help you.

Why some people think that stopping without help is the best way of doing it

A lot of people think that you are better off not seeking support for stopping and that the best way to do it is just to decide to stop and get on with it. Frankly, that is not generally true. Getting expert advice with stopping smoking, just like many other things in life, can make all the difference.

One argument against using support that you will hear sometimes goes like this: 'More people have stopped by not using some kind of support or medicine than have stopped with it, so stopping without support must be better.'

There are two very big reasons why this argument is wrong. First, it is true that there is a higher number of people who succeed in stopping without support. However, many more people actually *try* to stop without support than with it – and the *proportion* succeeding without support is lower. So even though not as many succeed out of those who try, there are so many smokers trying that it still adds up to a big number. If everyone who tried to give up smoking were using the most effective methods, we would have hundreds of thousands more people breaking free from smoking.

Secondly, the smokers who typically use support tend to be more nicotine-dependent. They have probably tried to stop many times without, and that is why they are using support – which makes perfect sense. So we are comparing chalk and cheese.

In my research, once we'd factored in how nicotine-dependent smokers were, we found that those who used support from the NHS Stop Smoking Services were *three times more likely* to achieve lasting success than those who tried without any support.

Ingredient 4: Professional stop-smoking advisor

Rating: ★ ★ ★

Support from a stop-smoking advisor typically involves weekly sessions lasting up to an hour, starting before your quit date and going on for at least four weeks after that date.

There are more than 80 high-quality studies showing that seeing a stop-smoking advisor hugely increases your chances of lasting success at stopping compared with just brief advice from a health professional or a booklet. This is true for one-to-one support and group programmes.

The Story of the Stop Smoking Service

When I started studying smoking way back in 1982 there was almost nothing for the large majority of smokers who wanted help giving up. Your doctor might have advised you to stop, but from there on you'd be on your own. No help, no support, nothing.

This was a terrible shame because we had good evidence, even back then, that professional advice was helpful to smokers wanting to stop. My colleagues and I tried to get the government to provide this kind of support for over a decade with no luck.

But when a Labour government was elected in the UK in 1997, one of its priorities was trying to reduce the inequalities in health between the rich and the poor. And the main cause of that was smoking: poorer people tended to smoke and richer people tended not to. That was the main reason poorer people were dying earlier. (A very important study done in Scotland has shown that rich smokers die younger than poor non-smokers – and poor smokers die youngest of all.)

So the government decided to publish the first-ever national strategy of any country in the world to tackle smoking.

At that time I was working at St George's Hospital Medical School, and my friend and colleague Dr Martin Raw was working in the Institute of Psychiatry. Martin had been commissioned by the Health Education Authority (a government body whose job it was to help people achieve healthy lifestyles) to write guidelines for health professionals on stopping smoking. Originally it was going to take the form of a leaflet for health professionals. But we already knew that those leaflets were a complete waste of time. There had been a study done in the 1980s which had sent leaflets on smoking to every GP in the country. A few months later they asked the GPs what they thought of the leaflets; the vast majority of the GPs didn't even know they'd been sent them!

We needed these guidelines to be taken seriously – so we started looking around for support. We got a huge list of top medical organisations to back the guidelines – including the Royal College of Physicians, the Royal College of General Practitioners and the Royal College of Nursing. So in the end our guidelines were incorporated into the ground-breaking national strategy.

The upshot was that in 1998, for the first time anywhere in the world, Britain set up its national Stop Smoking Service.

The idea was simple: any smoker in the country who wanted help stopping smoking could go to their GP and ask for a referral to this stop-smoking service.

When it first started up it treated about 100,000 people each year, which seemed like a massive number at the time. In 2012, it treated more than 700,000 people – which is almost one in ten smokers. Since the service started it's saved many thousands of lives, and it's one of the largest and most important parts of the health service today – all in just over ten years.

It was set up as a free service to help smokers. There is no catch. It's paid for out of taxes because it's a fantastic way to improve the health of the population.

And generally the advisors are incredibly understanding and supportive. There is no nagging and they are not in the least bit judgemental. I mention this because I know that a lot of smokers are put off seeing a stop-smoking advisor because they think they will be 'told off', and when they do finally go it is a really nice surprise to receive such a friendly welcome.

I know that sometimes in our health system you turn up to see your local doctor or nurse and you get the sense they'd rather you had stayed at home (especially if you have a stinking cold!). This isn't the case for the stop-smoking advisors. They're delighted to see you and are keen to help. They know that if they help you to quit, they might have saved your life. And if that wasn't enough, their organisation gets paid for how many people they treat and how many successes they have. If you blow into their carbon monoxide breath test machine after four weeks and prove you haven't been smoking, not only do they get a warm glow in their hearts, they also get more money.

The UK's Stop Smoking Service has now been copied in more than 40 countries around the world. But I think we still have the most complete coverage of any country.

Finding a stop-smoking advisor

The easiest way to find your local NHS Stop Smoking Service is to visit (or phone) your GP and ask for a referral. However, you don't need a referral – if you see a poster or a leaflet advertising the service you can call them directly. Or in England you can go to the NHS

SmokeFree website: <http://smokefree.nhs.uk>. In Wales you go to <www.stopsmokingwales.com>. In Scotland go to <www.canstop smoking.com>. If you are in Northern Ireland call the Helpline on 0808 812 8008.

How does stop-smoking support work?

If you get good, high-quality professional support, that will be massively useful to help you stop smoking. But how does it work and what will it be like?

Let's look at why it helps. The first thing is that it's really useful to have someone else to talk to about how you are getting on – whether it's in a group or talking one-on-one to a practitioner. Having someone else involved in a professional way provides an additional motivation to stop. So if you slip up, you're not just letting yourself down – you now feel you're either letting down the group or the practitioner. And if it's a good practitioner, they'll establish a good relationship with you in which they care about your quit attempt. That helps a lot.

The second thing is that the stop-smoking advisor can give you lots of very good practical advice on things you can do to avoid cravings and how to deal with them when they arise. For example, they can discuss your daily routine with you and identify situations where you would normally smoke. And they can help you select the situations which – at least for a while – you can avoid or change.

So, for instance, if you travel to work by bus, and you'd normally smoke at the bus stop then that bus stop is now a cue for you to light up. That means you'll find it a bit of a struggle when you go to that bus stop and you'll probably want to have a cigarette. Your practitioner will then suggest some options:

1 Can you take a different route to work? Can you find another bus stop? (So basically avoiding the situation.)
2 If there's somewhere you normally stand at that bus stop, stand in a different place.

It's really basic in a way, because the bit of your brain that is giving you the urges to smoke is not the clever part. It's the stupid part. So, even if you're just facing in a different direction, it means you're exposed to different stimuli – so you shouldn't get such strong cravings.

I'll tell you more about changing your routines when we get to Ingredient 19. In fact, a good advisor will talk to you about a lot of the things I cover in this book. The difference, of course, is that an advisor can work carefully with you to develop your own plan that really suits your needs. They'll use the same information I do, but they can really personalise it.

It's very important that your advisor should see you at least once a week. The meetings should start from before the point at which you set your quit date, to at least four weeks afterwards. The reason for that is that the first four weeks are when the cravings and withdrawal symptoms are at their worst. Their job is to get you over that initial hump. Obviously they can't see you forever, but they can get you on your way. And having that structure, knowing that you're going to be seeing this person in a week's time, can help keep you motivated.

Another thing they do is to measure the concentration of carbon monoxide in your breath (see the box below). Your advisor should show you your readings and discuss with you exactly what they mean. Before you quit, they should explain that when you come back after stopping your reading should be the same as any non-smoker.

If your CO reading is high and you really and truly haven't smoked, they will be able to advise you on what might be causing it. It's just possible that you have been exposed very heavily to a smoky atmosphere, but these days that's extremely unlikely. More likely is that you have a faulty gas fire in your house or a leaky exhaust in your car. So you should check those out immediately.

Your advisor will tell you that from the moment you have your last cigarette, your CO level will start to come down quite rapidly. The 'half-life', as it's called, is about three hours. That means that every three hours the concentration of carbon monoxide in the blood halves. So if you start with a level of twenty, after three hours it will be ten, then three hours after that it will be five and so on. That means that when you come back to see them, if you haven't smoked, then you will have the same level of carbon monoxide as a non-smoker. And they'll be able to tell that from the breathalyser and show you the benefits you're getting immediately from not

The carbon monoxide breath test

When you smoke a cigarette you inhale tar particles, nicotine and a gas called carbon monoxide (CO). CO is not to be confused with carbon dioxide (CO_2), which is what you normally exhale when you breathe. Both are produced when you burn anything that has carbon in it, such as paper, petrol, coal, oil or tobacco. But CO is deadly poisonous!

When you inhale cigarette smoke, CO gets into your blood stream via your lungs. Once there, it attaches itself to your red blood cells, knocking off the oxygen that the cells are supposed to be carrying. So when people die from carbon monoxide poisoning, they are really dying from asphyxiation.

Fortunately for you, the amount you inhale from cigarettes isn't anything like enough to asphyxiate you. But it *is* hardening your arteries. Your stop-smoking advisor can use the CO breath test to tell whether you have been smoking recently and how much smoke you have been inhaling.

When you have your breath tested, the adviser will get you to hold your breath for about 15 seconds. During that time the CO from your blood goes into your lungs. Then you empty your lungs into the CO monitor and it uses the amount of CO in the air you breathe out to tell you how much was in your blood.

Typical readings for smokers are 10–30 parts per million. Typical readings for non-smokers are less than ten parts per million and usually less than five parts per million.

Your reading will come down to a normal non-smoking level within a day of stopping, so your stop-smoking advisor can use this to see whether you really are smoking or not and how heavy a smoker you are.

Sometimes smokers get a little worried after they have stopped because the reading isn't zero. They say, 'I haven't smoked, honestly!' However everyone has some carbon monoxide in their blood, as I have already explained – as long as it is less than ten parts per million that is fine.

Fig 8.1 Smoker blowing into a CO monitor

smoking. You'll find it a real feel-good moment when you go in to have your breath tested and you come out with a low reading. It's a big boost.

Very importantly, the stop-smoking practitioner will advise you on what nicotine products or stop-smoking medicine you should take (see ingredients 10, 11, 12, 13 and 14). If you meet a good stop-smoking practitioner, they will strongly advise you to use some form of medicine to help you stop. That's because it makes a big difference to your chances of success.

It's not necessary – a lot of people stop without them – but, particularly if you smoke more than ten cigarettes a day, it is strongly recommended that you use one or more forms of medicine. What the practitioner can do, like I do in this book, is to explain to you how the medicines work. But because they'll be right there in front of you, they can discuss with you which medicines might be suitable and can help you consider the pros and cons.

Also, if you're experiencing side effects, or there's anything that concerns you, they can reassure you, or they can tell you about what to expect in the future.

So a good stop-smoking practitioner will do a lot of the things that are in this book, but with the added advantage that it's an interaction with another human being. However, one of the things you should know is that there's quite wide variation in the skills and knowledge of the different practitioners. Also, the stop-smoking service that they work for may have different procedures. The next section tells you what I think, from the research evidence, your stop-smoking practitioner should do with you. It's quite detailed so you can skip it if you like, but at least it will always be there if you want to refer to it.

What should the sessions be like?

A good stop-smoking course should involve at least six visits, starting a week or two before the target quit date and continuing for at least four weeks after that date.

Here is what I would expect a good stop-smoking advisor to do at each visit.

First visit

At your first visit your advisor should do the following:

1   Greet you warmly and respectfully and make you feel welcome.
2   Explain the course you are embarking on, what you are expected to do and how it will help, making it clear that he or she is there to help and support you, not to tell you off or try to scare you into stopping; your advisor is on your side and with you every step of the way.
3   Find out about what is motivating you to stop, what you have done in the past to try to stop and what you think took you back to smoking, then discuss with you how you can learn from these experiences.
4   Measure your expired-air carbon monoxide level using the simple breath test, and explain the results in a way that can help you understand the immediate benefits you will get when you stop.
5   Explain about available nicotine-replacement products and stop-smoking medicines (see chapters 10 and 11) and strongly encourage you to use one; ideally they should be able to provide the products for you.
6   Get you to commit to a definite quit date as soon as possible and normally within the next two weeks.
7   Advise you not to make an effort to cut down, just smoke normally until your quit date, but to start taking whatever medicine you are taking a week before that date (unless of course the date is today).
8   Discuss with you ways in which you may be able to change your routines and other activities for the first few weeks to minimise your exposure to smoking triggers.
9   Discuss with you how to cope with any difficult situations that might be coming up, and the importance of thinking like a non-smoker; emphasising that after the quit date you must do everything you possibly can to avoid even a single puff on your cigarette. Your maxim must be: not a puff, no matter what.
10 Check that you are still feeling committed to stopping on the target quit date.
11 Ask you if you have any questions or concerns and make sure you have plenty of opportunity to talk about these, answering any factual questions.

12 Set a date for your next session, which will normally be your tar-get quit date, and give you an appointment card to remind you.

Second visit

At the second visit, which will normally be on your quit date, your stop-smoking advisor should:

1 Greet you warmly and respectfully and be genuinely pleased that you have made it to this important day in your life.
2 Ask you how things have been going since the last visit.
3 Take a CO reading and explain that once you have stopped that reading will come down to a non-smoker level and you will be able to see this when you return. (If you have already stopped that morning the reading will already be down.)
4 Check that you have managed to get your medicine, if appropri-ate. Ask if you have been taking it and whether you have had any untoward reactions.
5 Check that you are still committed to quitting today.
6 Confirm your commitment to the 'not a puff' rule.
7 Confirm your plans for how you are going to avoid the smoking triggers and exactly what you are going to do when you get urges to smoke in different situations.
8 Make sure that you have your supplies of nicotine products or medicines and that you understand the importance of using these properly – not stopping before the end of the course and making sure that you use enough to make a difference.
9 Point you in the direction of useful resources on the Internet, if you have access to it.
10 Go through the typical nicotine-withdrawal symptoms with you and make sure you know what to expect and have a plan for coping with it.
11 Set a date for the next session which will normally be in a week's time and say how much he or she is looking forward to you com-ing back and reporting that you have not smoked at all for the past week and showing a nice low CO reading.

Further visits

Your advisor will want you to come back after the target quit date – *whether or not you have managed to stay off cigarettes*. Please don't stay away out of embarrassment. And remember, you have not failed – there is no such thing as failure when it comes to trying to stop smoking. Whatever happens, you have made progress.

Sure, you have set yourself a goal of 'not a puff' no matter what. And that is important. But if you do have a puff, or even just carry on smoking, it is not the end of the road – it just means that another tack is needed. Your advisor will recognise that you may not have made it even past the first day but he or she will be with you for as long as it takes to help you succeed for good.

So at each of the visits after your target quit date, your advisor should:

1 Thank you for coming back and make you feel welcome.
2 Ask how you have been getting on and ask whether you have smoked at all during the last week. If you have smoked, perhaps just one or two cigarettes, it is important to tell your advisor because then they can give you important advice on how to avoid this happening again.
3 Express real pleasure and shower praise on you for not smoking.
4 Take a CO reading and explain to you the results – even if you have not smoked all week your level will almost certainly not be zero, because even non-smokers have some CO in their bodies from things like inhaling car exhaust fumes and even from their own body's production of CO when red blood cells are replaced.
5 Ask you about how you have been feeling generally, and try to find out whether your morale might be getting a little low.
6 Ask about use of your nicotine product or medicine and whether you are getting any untoward reactions that need discussing.
7 Ask about any difficult situations you encountered and what you did to deal with them so that you can remember to use a similar approach next time.
8 Ask you how you feel about the week ahead and whether there is anything coming up that could put pressure on you – be it a party, an evening out with friends or a stressful meeting at work.
9 Discuss how you are going to deal with whatever is coming up in the week ahead.

10 Ask you how the goal of starting to think like a non-smoker is coming along.

11 Ask if you have any questions or concerns and give you plenty of time to discuss these.

12 Set a date, usually in a week's time for your next visit (unless this is your last visit) and say how much he or she is looking forward to you reporting that you have not smoked at all.

Again, I can't stress enough how important it is to come back – whatever happens. Your advisor won't tell you off if you have smoked but will help you put into action a plan to get back on track. If you have decided that this quit attempt is over, then all you have to do is call and let them know.

It's also really important that you go back and see your advisor each week, even if everything is going fine. So many times, I've known people who are trying to stop thinking that everything is going great – no worries – and then, suddenly: bam – they are hit by something. It could be an argument at home, a stressful day at work, a party, or just nothing in particular – and they are struggling. Continuing to see your stop-smoking advisor, even when things are going well, will provide an important buffer for you when this happens and could make all the difference.

The target culture

Some places will allow you to go in person at first and then continue support over the phone. That may be fine except that you won't be able to get your CO reading. At some point, though, they should ask you back in to take the CO test to check you haven't been smoking.

Please go. It may not feel crucial for you, but it is for them – and for all the other smokers trying to quit in future. It's an unfortunate fact of life in Britain today that it's not enough to do something – you have to be able to prove you've done it. Unless you go back and prove that you haven't smoked they can't claim you as a success and their funding will be at risk.

On a more positive note it's really nice for them when you come back and blow into their CO monitor. We all need to feel we are doing some good in our working lives and I can tell you that it's such a great feeling to know that you have helped someone to stop smoking. Stop-smoking advisors don't get paid much – they do it for the love of it – so let's give them the reward they deserve.

Group Sessions

Some stop-smoking services will offer you a choice between seeing someone one-to-one – or perhaps with your partner or a friend – or joining a stop-smoking group. A lot of people immediately say things like: 'I want to be seen on my own', 'What's the group going to do?', 'Am I going to have to stand up and do embarrassing things?' and 'Will I get the same level of attention as I would in a one-to-one session?'

The research tells us that people who go to the groups tend to be more successful. I think the most important reason for that is the way the groups are run enables you to form a relationship with the group where no one wants to let each other down. So it provides a stronger barrier against your going back to smoking.

This is certainly what the people who attend the groups say. They were going to have a cigarette but then think: 'When I blow into the carbon monoxide machine everyone will see that I've been smoking.' Or: 'If I don't turn up because I'm too embarrassed, everyone will know I've slipped up.' Or: 'I'll have to get up in front of the group and admit that I've been smoking.' That feeling of letting other people down is very unpleasant. Funnily enough, people really like the fact that that's what kept them motivated.

People also find that the groups are much more fun than they thought they would be. You might think that a roomful of tetchy smokers all trying to quit at the same time sounds a bit grim, but in fact well-run groups are more like a friendly pleasant group chat. The good ones tend not to involve the specialist in the conversation very much. It's smokers talking to each other, sharing experiences, giving each other advice from their own experience and giving each other encouragement and support. This is potentially more powerful than getting it from the stop-smoking health professional. So I would advise anyone to give it a go if there's a group available.

You might be put off by the image you have of Alcoholics Anonymous meetings. Don't worry: it's not like that at all (although these have been found to be very helpful in combating alcohol dependence). The support that's given to smokers is different from support given for other addictions. The Stop Smoking Service in the UK assumes that there is nothing wrong with you. They assume that you're just like anyone else, except you happen to be addicted to nicotine from cigarettes, so their job is to help you solve that problem.

It's not about getting deep into your psyche, or changing you as a person, or converting you to a religion. There's no psychoanalysis or anything like that. The problem is simple: you're addicted to cigarettes, and when you try to stop you experience powerful urges and withdrawal symptoms which drive you back to smoking. They ask what they can do to reduce those urges, help you to get through them without smoking so you can come out the other side free. It's more like an exercise class or going to see a financial advisor.

Another thing about groups is that a lot of people think that maybe a small group would be better than a big one. The evidence is actually that the big groups tend to do better than the small groups. A good size for a group is anything from 15–30 people. Everyone sits round in a circle talking to each other. It makes for a very lively, energetic, fun occasion. No one is forced to say anything, but what's very interesting is that in a well-run group everyone feels comfortable enough to talk. You have a talking point immediately, which is that you all want to quit smoking.

What about attending an Allen Carr 'Easyway' session?

Allen Carr's 'Easyway' course is widely publicised and very popular – you may have tried this approach. It involves a single session (though you can go back if it doesn't work the first time) which is aimed at getting you to think differently about smoking. The goal is to help you convince yourself that there is no earthly reason why you should want to smoke. The courses and books keep repeating the message that smoking is doing nothing for you and once you truly realise this it's easy to stop.

I can only give you my opinion on this because there haven't been the RCTs (Randomised Control Trials, see page 90) needed to back this up, but I think this approach can be effective if you are someone who can truly buy into it. But I also think there are a few things that you will need to think about if you decide this is something you want to try. One is that you might not be able to convince yourself that you don't want to smoke. If you are experiencing strong urges to smoke, despite all your mental efforts, you will need other ingredients to keep you away from cigarettes.

Leading stop-smoking advisors answer your questions

I asked several of the country's leading stop-smoking advisors, including Dr Andy McEwen, who heads the organisation that trains and assesses them (see <http://www.ncsct.co.uk>), a few questions on your behalf. This is a compilation of what they told me.

Q *What should I expect from my stop-smoking advisor?*

A A good advisor will talk with you in a way that's relaxed and non-judgmental. We work hard to build a connection with the smokers who come to see us. We listen carefully and ask questions to get you thinking about coming up with solutions for yourself. If an advisor is working incredibly hard – singing, dancing and doing jazz hands – it makes the smoker quite passive. We give you our expertise, but you need to be the master of your quit attempt.

Q *What will the advisor expect of me?*

A It's important to understand you're not coming in for a one-off appointment to just get some patches and see how it goes. It's a free service, but we expect you to come back and see us on a regular basis. And even if you've had a slip, we're there to support you. We realise it can be difficult and we don't tell people off for slipping up; we take a more empathetic approach, which works a lot better.

Q *Can I use medication as well?*

A Yes, and we reassure clients that the medication is safe because there's still lots of myths around them. For example, some people are worried the patches might give them cancer, but that isn't true. So we explain the difference between patches and cigarettes: you're exchanging a cigarette, which contains lots of dangerous chemicals, for a safe alternative.

Q *Will I feel judged?*

A Not at all. Most people say they're pleasantly surprised when they find out we're not judgmental and don't wag our fingers at them. Quite the opposite: we're very pleased that you're serious about making the effort to stop.

Q *Am I wasting the advisor's time?*

A Again, absolutely not. Some people feel that seeking professional help might be a waste of someone else's time. Although they realise it's something they need to stop doing, they feel like they should be able to do it on their own without help. But we know how hard it is and that's why the service was set up. So there's no need for you to worry about wasting our time: we're here to support you.

Q *Deep down I'm not sure I can quit, can you still help?*

A A lot of people feel like they're a lost cause. But we've had lots of people over the years who have been heavily addicted and still managed to quit. Many people tell themselves they can't stop and that becomes a self-fulfilling prophecy. There's absolutely no reason why you can't quit, but you've got to tell yourself that you can. We can help you get to that point.

Q *What are the group sessions like?*

A The group stop-smoking sessions are very powerful. In the first session we ask everyone to give the reason why they've come to the session. People say things like: 'Oh, I've had a scan and I might have throat cancer', 'My children hate the smoking', 'I've got a baby on the way' and so on. We tell them they'll need to remember this reason over the coming weeks. We give them a wristband that says 'remember why'. It gives them something to fiddle around with but hopefully it reinforces the message: remember why you came here and what's important to you.

I find that most people really benefit from quitting in groups. This is because you get a group of people who are going through the whole experience together. All we're asking for is six to seven hours of your lives, and we'll massively improve your chances of quitting, which will save you lots of money and potentially give you 20 to 30 years of extra life.

Q *What will I do in each session?*

A We do a one-hour session once a week over six to seven weeks. The first session is an introductory session where we get everyone to talk about why they want to quit smoking. We like to ask them how they got started, because that illustrates the power of groups nicely. Most people start when they're teenagers because of peer pressure. So we like to say: 'Groups got you into smoking – groups are going to get you out!' And then we talk briefly about the medications and get people to set a quit date.

In the second week we go into the medications in some detail and ask them about previous quit attempts. Throughout the programme we really emphasise the 'not a single puff' rule.

In the third week we get them to quit. We buddy them up with another member of the group and have a betting game: they put their money in an envelope with their buddy and if they smoke they lose their buddy's money as well. So that's another small barrier between them and smoking. And we also ask them to make a promise to the group that they won't smoke for the next seven days.

And they just come back each week, report their progress, tell people how they're getting on and share their experiences. And three or four weeks after the quit date it's becoming a lot easier – they're starting to feel the benefits, and they've got through the worst of the withdrawal symptoms.

We always have a small celebration at the final session. We have some food and the advisor might bring a couple of bottles of wine. At the end of the sessions, most of the people are really thankful for the group and say it's the one of the main things that helped them to quit.

Q *Will coming to the Stop Smoking Service boost my chances of success?*

A If you look at the figures, coming to a stop-smoking service is obviously a good thing to do. But ultimately the motivation has to come from you. The stop-smoking service just provides empathetic, structured support for your attempt. It's almost like you're building the wall, but we're providing a little bit of scaffolding. So maybe without us, certain sections of the wall would get a bit shaky and fall down. Sometimes just knowing we're here tends to help people in their weaker moments and keep them smokefree.

Secondly, the Allen Carr method strongly advises you not to use any of the stop-smoking medicines. This concerns me: these medicines have been shown in lots of high-quality RCTs to improve your chances of quitting. I understand why the approach advises against these medicines. The whole point is that stopping is easy once you truly believe that smoking is not doing anything for you – so you shouldn't need medicines. But the fact is that these medicines have been tested very many times in RCTs. If it were a treatment for lung cancer I would definitely go for the one that had RCT evidence behind it. I do not agree that the ingredient on which the Allen Carr method focuses actually rules out using medication if that turns out to be helpful.

Finally, I do worry about the fact that you have to pay for the courses. I know that many smokers don't have a lot of money and it is quite a large outlay – especially when you can go to an NHS stop-smoking advisor for nothing.

So I'm certainly not advising you against paying for an Allen Carr course. A lot of smokers have been on it and swear by it. But at least you know my opinion on whether it is likely to help you. And if you decide to try it, I suggest that you use it as one of your ingredients – *not the only one*.

What about hypnotherapy?

Hypnotherapy involves using the power of suggestion to get you to think that you don't want or need to smoke any more. It is using a specific technique to do what the Allen Carr method does using persuasion. You will probably have to pay for it.

There has been very little research, but a few small RCTs found it to increase lasting success rates compared with just a brief chat, but it was not found to be more effective than an equivalent amount of time giving you general psychological support.

In Chapter 6 I used hypnotherapy to show what kind of evidence was helpful in deciding what ingredients to use in your stop-smoking formula. Let me explain this a bit more. Hypnotherapy involves the 'power of suggestion'. We are all more or less suggestible – even those of us who think we aren't. I probably am. If I see someone drinking whisky in a film, I find myself wanting one – and I don't even like whisky! And sometimes we are more suggestible than other times. Hypnotherapy aims to get you to a point where statements made by the hypnotherapist are taken as true and commands are obeyed, without question.

Imagine if I could truly get you to believe that the next cigarette you smoked would kill you stone dead immediately. You wouldn't smoke it. Or if I got you to know in your heart that smoking did absolutely nothing for you – it was just a total waste of money. Or that cigarettes tasted of dog excrement. You would stop smoking (probably).

The problem with all this, obviously, is that hypnotherapy is mostly not as powerful as some would like to believe. But that is not to say that it might not have some use in this case. Some people are more suggestible than others. Stage hypnotists perform a few simple routines to find out which members of their audience will be suitable to be made a fool of by getting them to cluck like a chicken, or crawl like a baby!

Here's a classic one: close your eyes and hold your arms out in front of you. Then imagine holding a stack of books on your left hand, while a bunch of helium balloons is tied to your right hand. Really think about the forces pulling your left hand down and pushing your right hand up. Go on – do it now, and then after 20 seconds open your eyes.

What happened when you opened your eyes? Was your right hand way above your left? The further apart they are, the more suggestible you're likely to be. (The psychologist Richard Wiseman has a nice little video of this you can easily find online – just search for 'Richard Wiseman: are you prone to mind control'. It's not a full suggestibility test but you might find it instructive.)

There are loads of other tests like this on the Internet – just google 'suggestibility tests for hypnotists'.

Anyway, if you are seriously considering using a hypnotherapist, here are a couple of questions you can ask him or her to help you decide whether to go ahead:

1 How many people have you hypnotised in the past 12 months in an effort to help them stop smoking?
2 How many of them have you followed up at least four weeks later to find out whether they stopped and did not smoke again?
3 And how many of these do you know for sure were not smoking because you got them to blow into a CO monitor and they provided a reading of less than ten parts per million?

Don't let them get away with saying that 90 per cent (or whatever) of their customers were satisfied, or 60 per cent of those who they managed to contact said they were not smoking – that doesn't tell you what you need to know. Under the rules of this particular game, everyone they can't get to blow into their CO machine to prove they have given up must be counted as still smoking. That may seem harsh, but it is what the free NHS services have to do. And I imagine that you wouldn't want to pay for something that is less effective than a service you could get for free.

Ingredient 5: Telephone helpline

Rating: ★ ★ ★

RCTs tell us for sure that calling a telephone helpline can help you stop, although it depends on the particular helpline you call, how well the advisors are trained and how you use it.

Ideally you should set up a string of calls taking you through at least the first four weeks of abstinence. The advisor on the other end of the line should quickly set a quit date with you, advise you about using a stop-smoking medicine or nicotine product, help you set up clear ground rules about how you are going to approach the quit attempt and give you clear advice about how to deal with the problems you are likely to encounter. The advisor should be supportive and encouraging, adopting a friendly but professional manner.

I told you in the last section that face-to-face support from a trained advisor can help you to stop. You can also get professional support on the telephone by phoning a helpline. The organisation QUIT (<http://www.quit.org.uk>) provides a helpline for some of the local stop-smoking services. Also anyone in the UK can phone a National Health helpline (England: 0800 022 4 332; Wales: 0800 085 2219; Scotland: 0800 848 484; Northern Ireland: 0800 783 3339); the person on the other end will ask you whether you want to be put in touch with your local service for face-to-face support, speak to an advisor by phone or just receive some written materials.

Obviously it's much more convenient to get your support on the phone, and you may have the option of being able to call up during working hours any time you feel you need a booster.

I would expect a good telephone counsellor to do almost everything a good face-to-face counsellor would do. The downside is that you may not get the same kind of relationship with the person as you would face-to-face, and in fact you may not speak to the same person each time. There's no way round that, but they should be able to sort out other practical problems.

For example, the advisor should be able to send you nicotine products if you decide to use one, or send you a voucher to get them from a pharmacy. Alternatively they could send you to your GP to get a prescription for one of the medicines. They might also ask you to visit a local pharmacist or health centre a couple of times to measure your CO levels.

Some people prefer the convenience or anonymity of talking on the phone; others find it's just not the same. Given the choice, I personally would opt for face-to-face sessions, but phone services are a good option if you can't find a good stop-smoking advisor in your area or prefer the convenience of speaking to someone from the comfort of your own home.

Chapter 9

Automated Support and Self-help Materials

If you have a smartphone or ready access to the Internet, you will probably have looked at quite a few websites and apps that aim to help you stop smoking. You may have picked up a booklet from your local surgery or hospital. Or you may have bought one of the popular books on stopping smoking, such as *Allen Carr's Easy Way to Stop Smoking*.

I am now going to give you the low-down on all these ingredients. I'll tell you which ones have strong evidence to back them up and which ones are less well supported.

As always, remember that it's your choice: I guide – you decide.

Ingredient 6: Text-messaging programme

Rating: ★ ★ ★

Text-messaging programmes, such as the one you can sign up to from the NHS SmokeFree website (<http://http://smokefree.nhs.uk>), send you frequent text messages, giving you helpful tips and encouragement. The simplest way to sign up is to text TXTHELP to 63818. A very large RCT of a programme called Txt2stop showed that it doubled long-term success rates, and there are some other smaller studies showing the same thing.

It is possible that other text-messaging services are not as effective, but if they follow a similar programme to the Txt2stop service that was tested, there is every reason to believe they would help.

NHS Quit Smoking Txt2stop

I helped advise on a very large RCT that aimed to test the text-messaging service Txt2stop, which was developed at the London School of Hygiene and Tropical Medicine (one of the world's leading universities specialising in public health) based on an earlier one that had been developed in New Zealand.

While the study was going on, I have to confess I was not optimistic that Txt2stop would show any effect. I couldn't see how just receiving text messages would help very much. In fact you might imagine that they would make things worse by reminding you about smoking when you are trying to put it out of your mind. So it was a very nice surprise when the results came through that the smokers who had been randomly chosen to receive the Txt2stop messages were *twice as likely to stop* for at least six months as those who had been randomly chosen to receive text messages that talked more generally about health issues.

This was a very large study involving nearly 6,000 smokers, so there was no doubt at all that the result was genuine. And, unusually for a study of this kind, the study team had managed to get hold of almost everyone who had started the study and were able to check that those who said they were not smoking really were telling the truth by testing for nicotine by-products in their saliva.

This study was published in one of the world's top medical journals, *The Lancet*. (Here seems a good place to remind you that if you want to check up on any of these references for yourself, or have a look at any of the studies I talk about in this book, you can find details on the website <http://www.smokefreeformula.co.uk>.)

Professor Susan Michie and I, together with the lead researcher of that study, Dr Cari Free, carried out an in-depth analysis of the content of the text messages, and I think that perhaps one of the key things that they did was to ensure that the smokers *set a definite quit date* soon after joining the study. It then provided a kind of virtual buddy who was with the smokers during the difficult first few weeks

– always available and always encouraging them to keep them motivated.

You can't get this precise text-messaging service now, but the Department of Health has developed one based on it: NHS Quit Smoking, which you can get hold of simply by going to <http://smokefree.nhs.uk/ways-to-quit/support-on-your-mobile/> or text TXTHELP to 63818.

Ingredient 7: Stop-smoking website

Rating: ★ ★

Stop-smoking websites vary enormously. Several large RCTs have shown that they can increase your chances of lasting success. We do not know as much as we would like about what makes one site effective and another not, but if they follow a few basic rules, I think they should help.

When I put 'How to stop smoking' into Google I got over 129,000,000 hits! That gives you an idea as to how much information there is on the web aimed at helping you stop …

Unfortunately the number of RCTs evaluating stop-smoking websites can be counted on your fingers and toes. The good news is that there is reason to believe that there is something in some of these websites that can help you stop. The bad news is, whatever it is, lots of the stop-smoking websites don't have it!

What to look for in a website

So how do you pick which of the many websites to use? Well, I can tell you what elements I think you should probably look out for:

1 **Is it free?** There is no point in paying for a stop-smoking website when there are plenty of free ones available.
2 **Does it get you to set a firm quit date, and then give you a programme to follow after that date?** If you don't set a firm quit date, you won't quit. That date might be today, but it should at least be within the next couple of weeks. Anything longer than that and

you will probably have gone off the boil. Having a course for you to follow, and giving you a way of tracking your progress, is probably very important. It might help you calculate how much money you've saved, how many hours of life you've saved and so on. It might allow you to track your cravings so you can see that things are getting easier.

3 **Does it encourage you to use stop-smoking medicines?** One of the few pieces of hard evidence we have on how stop-smoking websites work is a study I was involved in a few years ago in which we tested a website called Click2Quit (there's a pattern to these names, isn't there?). This was set up by the drug company Glaxo-SmithKline for people using their nicotine products. As you can imagine, they were keen that the smokers used their products properly and didn't skimp. What we found was that one of the main ways that the website increased smokers' chances of stopping was by doing just that – helping them to use their nicotine product properly, using enough of it every day, and using it for long enough for it to work.

4 **Does it give you tailored advice on ways of avoiding or coping with urges to smoke?** Of course you can get advice like that from a book like this one, but what a website should be able to do is to ask you questions about difficult situations and give you very tailored advice based on your answers. It should also give you the option to receive text messages to remind you about the importance of not giving in to temptation at crucial moments.

5 **Does it use graphic imagery and activities to bring alive its content?** There is so much more that can be done using the Internet than you can't get from a book – videos, pretty pictures (or disgusting pictures!), games and so on.

The last point might not seem so crucial, but actually it's quite important. While there are computer games that are so engaging they get users totally hooked, websites aimed at helping people stay healthy struggle to get visitors to return. You don't have to be a psychologist to know why; as I pointed out in Part One, everything we do is driven by what we want or need to do at that precise moment. People who play games get caught up in the fantasy – the problem that they want to solve and the little successes they achieve almost every second. So at every moment when they are playing the game … they want to keep playing. And when they are not playing the game, they experience pleasure at the thought of resuming the game or starting a new one. The computer game industry is massive and it has learned how to keep its players hooked.

And then there is that fact that most games players are young people who like that kind of thing. I remember the first computer game I ever played. It was called Colossal Cave Adventure. It ran on a PDP-11 minicomputer, which cost about £50,000 back in 1982, and this is what it looked like:

```
.RUN ADV11

WELCOME TO ADVENTURE!!  WOULD YOU LIKE INSTRUCTIONS?


YES
SOMEWHERE NEARBY IS COLOSSAL CAVE, WHERE OTHERS HAVE FOUND
FORTUNES IN TREASURE AND GOLD, THOUGH IT IS RUMORED
THAT SOME WHO ENTER ARE NEVER SEEN AGAIN. MAGIC IS SAID
TO WORK IN THE CAVE.  I WILL BE YOUR EYES AND HANDS. DIRECT
ME WITH COMMANDS OF 1 OR 2 WORDS.
(ERRORS, SUGGESTIONS, COMPLAINTS TO CROWTHER)
(IF STUCK TYPE HELP FOR SOME HINTS)


YOU ARE STANDING AT THE END OF A ROAD BEFORE A SMALL BRICK
BUILDING . AROUND YOU IS A FOREST. A SMALL
STREAM FLOWS OUT OF THE BUILDING AND DOWN A GULLY.


GO IN
YOU ARE INSIDE A BUILDING, A WELL HOUSE FOR A LARGE SPRING.

THERE ARE SOME KEYS ON THE GROUND HERE.

THERE IS A SHINY BRASS LAMP NEARBY.

THERE IS FOOD HERE.

THERE IS A BOTTLE OF WATER HERE.
```

Just reading this text, which I got from Wikipedia, brings back happy memories of pressing N, E, S, or W to explore the colossal cave.

Okay, an imaginary world of caves that you can't actually see might not seem like much of a rival to Call of Duty. But it was pretty fancy for the early 1980s, and from there I graduated to graphic adventures like the hilarious Monkey Island and real-time strategy games like Warcraft II and Command & Conquer.

Why am I telling you this? Because now I don't do any of that. I got bored with it. (Okay, so I still play some of these games with a friend once a year on a boys' weekend … but that's it.) So nowadays I wouldn't want a website that looked like a shoot-'em-up. But I can see how that's exactly what would have drawn me in when I was younger.

So the website that is going to work for you may well differ depending on how old you are and what you enjoy. You might want to get involved in a kind of game to keep you off cigarettes or you might want some nicely illustrated accurate information.

Suggested sites

Now for a plug! My team of psychologists and web programmers, led by Dr Jamie Brown, has developed a website to help you stop smoking called StopAdvisor. It is free to use because its development was paid for by a consortium of government and health charities.

StopAdvisor is a computerised expert stop-smoking advisor. It is designed to be extremely convenient. You are taken through a four-week stop-smoking course, just as you would if you visited a real life stop-smoking advisor.

Below is a screenshot. One thing you will notice is the picture of a bridge … which has nothing to do with smoking. When designing the website we realised that people need to feel good when they visit it and beautiful pictures can help with that experience – so I looked out for some pictures that I thought just about everyone would like. To get started with this website simply go to: <http://www.stopadvisor.com>. The results of field trials of the website are looking promising. See <http://smokefreeformula.com> for updates.

Apart from StopAdvisor, I would have a look at the NHS Smokefree website: <http://www.smokefree.nhs.uk>. This will give you lots of useful tips and information about quitting and point you in the direction of other tools, such as a quit app and stress-busting MP3 downloads and a free box called the 'Quit Kit'. It also has some nice videos of smokers who have stopped.

Here is a screenshot. You will see that it is different from StopAdvisor in that it mainly provides you with information and tools that you might want to help you with quitting rather than actively taking you through your quitting journey.

Ingredient 8: Another stop-smoking book

Rating: ★ ★

The most popular stop-smoking books have not been tested in RCTs unfortunately, but others have and by and large they have been found to have a small but useful effect.

I have only given them two stars because the most popular ones have not been tested. Also I have a concern that some of them make outlandish claims for effectiveness and also try to stop you using other methods that have been tested and found to work, such as stop-smoking medicines.

Can a book help you stop smoking? Yes, it can. Otherwise I'd be wasting your time right now! But leave aside *The SmokeFree Formula* for a minute because it is a bit different. Books can provide useful tips and advice, just like a website or an app, and they can do it cheaply and conveniently.

The most popular books are not necessarily the best of course. I would be wary of books that make big claims and tell you not to do things that have good evidence to back them up. As I mentioned before, I think Allen Carr's approach could be helpful – but that he is wrong to advise against stop-smoking medicines.

Ingredient 9: Smartphone app

Rating: ★

There is every reason to think that a smartphone app would help you stop smoking, but it probably depends on the app and, at the time of writing, there are no published RCTs of any of the apps on the market. This situation will probably change soon though, so keep an eye on the SmokeFree Formula website (<http://www.smokefreeformula.com>) for updates.

Almost half of smokers in Britain have smartphones – iPhones, BlackBerries, Android phones and other devices that can also act as diaries and web browsers, take photos, record and play videos, and run programs and apps.

There are now more than 180 stop-smoking apps available just in iTunes (the Apple iPhone app store). None have been properly tested yet, but my team has conducted an analysis of what they try to do.

Most of them aim to give you some idea of your progress. Some do this simply by allowing you to keep track of how much you are saving, while others may also track your cravings or days since you quit. Some of them give you motivational messages telling you about the benefits of quitting and urging you to stick with it. Very few of them give any advice on the use of stop-smoking medicines however, which is a downside.

Suggested apps

My guess is that there are many different types of stop-smoking app that could help you, each working in a different way.

I have developed one called SF28 (SF stands for smokefree) that focuses on staying completely smoke-free for four weeks – the time when the urges to smoke and nicotine-withdrawal symptoms are at their worst. If you can last out for four weeks, you are not out of the woods, but your chances of never smoking again are more than five times better than when you started.

To help you achieve the goal of staying smokefree for 28 days, the app gives you a 'toolbox'. This includes:

- Advice on ways to adjust your lifestyle so you can avoid unnecessary exposure to smoking triggers.
- Inspirational testimonials from ex-smokers.
- Video clips of ex-smokers telling you what it was like for them at the point you're at now.
- Advice on what to do when the cravings strike.
- A distraction game.
- Advice on what stop-smoking medicine to use and how to get the best out of it.

Your smokefree progress is charted with stars, hearts and by travelling down a road towards a rainbow. A little bird sitting on a sign tells you how much money you have saved.

I have been collecting data from thousands of smokers using this app and many seem to find it helpful. I can't tell you for sure that it will help though, because I have not done the necessary RCT. But I'm working on it and will update you on this via the SmokeFree Formula website (<http://www.smokefreeformula.com>).

If you want to have a look at the app, just search for SF28 in the iTunes store or Google Play or go to <http://www.sf28.co.uk>.

Some apps are free and others you have to pay for. From my analysis of the apps so far, I don't think the ones you pay for are any better than the free ones. But if you see one you particularly like the look of, perhaps it's worth investing – after all, the cost is usually no more than a packet of cigarettes.

Chapter 10

Nicotine Products

This chapter is one of the most important in *The SmokeFree Formula*. You may think you know all about these products, but I suspect there is a lot you don't know. So here goes …

> I realise that you might not want to take a product containing nicotine to help you stop smoking, since that is the drug you are trying to get off. If that is the case, then please bear with me. I'm not going to try to sell you anything, but I want to make sure you know the facts so you can decide for yourself.

Nicotine products cannot make you want to stop smoking, and they cannot stop you smoking. What they do is to reduce the power of the urges to smoke and the unpleasant withdrawal symptoms, letting your willpower do its work. Think back to the 'rider and the horse' model of the human brain I told you about in Chapter 2. Nicotine products are one of the most effective methods we have of taming the animal part of our brain – allowing the real you to take charge.

There are two main kinds of nicotine product to consider – those that we call 'licensed nicotine products' and 'electronic cigarettes'.

I'll tell you everything you need to know about both of these. Research is still going on, so things can change, but this is the most up-to-date information available. Keep an eye on the SmokeFree Formula website (<http://www.smokefreeformula.com>) for updates.

Ingredient 10: Licensed nicotine product

> ## Rating: ★ ★ ★
>
> Licensed nicotine products include nicotine gum, skin patches, lozenges, nasal sprays, inhalers and mouth sprays. In Britain you can either buy them from a shop or go to the doctor and get a prescription.
>
> The products typically give you less nicotine than from cigarettes and give it more slowly so they are much less addictive. Don't worry about taking too much either – the worst that will happen is you'll feel sick.
>
> There are vast numbers of RCTs showing that they increase your chances of stopping for at least a year by somewhere between 50 and 100 per cent if they are used as directed.
>
> But be warned: 'real world' studies tell us that many smokers who use nicotine products do not use as much as they need to or stay on them for long enough and end up getting little benefit from them. If you are going to use a nicotine product and you are not going to use professional support, you have to commit right from the start to using it properly – after all, you really do want to stop smoking.
>
> You should get the biggest effect if you start using a skin patch a couple of weeks before you stop smoking and then add one of the other products such as the gum, lozenge or inhaler. You then carry on using this combination for at least six weeks.

As my mentor, Professor Michael Russell, used to say: smokers smoke for the nicotine but die from the tar. Nicotine products are a very safe way of making that switch from being a smoker to being a non-smoker – a kind of stepping stone.

You may think that smoking is purely psychological, but that isn't true. If tobacco companies removed all traces of nicotine from cigarettes, almost no one would smoke them.

Nicotine products and nicotine addiction

Some people think it's bad to use nicotine products because it keeps you addicted. Even if this were true, it would still be much safer to be hooked on patches or gum, which contain no tar, than on cigarettes. But in fact these products deliver *much less nicotine than cigarettes and release it more slowly*, so most people do not become addicted. Cigarettes are so addictive because they give such a rapid nicotine hit. It's like the difference between chewing leaves from the coca plant and smoking crack cocaine.

The licensed nicotine products available in Britain right now are (in the order in which they were first marketed):

- Chewing gum
- Skin patch (also called transdermal patch)
- Nasal spray
- Inhaler (inhalator)
- Lozenge and mini-lozenge
- Mouth spray
- Dissolvable oral film

There is no evidence that one of these is better than any other over-all – some will suit some smokers better than others. But I will say that to get maximum effect *you should use a patch alongside one of the others* – the evidence for this is strong.

The thing to remember about licensed nicotine products is that, if you overdose, the worst that is going to happen is that you will feel sick and perhaps get a bit sweaty and clammy. Then you just reduce your dose again and you will be fine.

Now I am going to run through the different nicotine products that are available, with a short description for each one to show what it is, how it works, how you use it and what side effects to look out for. I suggest you start by reading what I have to say about nicotine gum, because a lot of the same ideas keep cropping up with the other products. Then take your pick …

Nicotine chewing gum

Nicotine gum was the first nicotine product licensed to help people stop smoking, and it is still one of the most popular ways of taking nicotine – being used by about a million smokers in Britain each year.

My very first study on smoking was testing the effect of nicotine gum on craving and withdrawal symptoms when compared with an inactive placebo. That was back in 1982.

Nicotine gum is a form of chewing gum (obviously), usually sugar-free, in which nicotine has been cleverly attached to the stuff you chew so that it is released slowly as your teeth compress it.

It is actually incredibly complex. You can't just mix the nicotine in with ordinary chewing gum because you won't get the controlled release that you need and it will taste disgusting. That is why the invention of nicotine gum was no mean feat and has transformed the lives of smokers across the world. You may think I'm exaggerating, but it paved the way for other nicotine therapies and I think it is one of the most important medical breakthroughs of the last 50 years.

Nicotine gum comes in doses up to four milligrams. I remember when the four-milligram gum first came to my lab for testing – it was pretty horrible. But now, even as an ex-smoker, I find it perfectly chewable. If you are going to use nicotine gum, I would recommend trying this first and only stepping down to two milligrams if you find it makes you feel sick.

There are now quite a lot of flavours and makes. I would tend to go for the cheapest because there is no particular reason to pay more.

Most smokers think they don't need instructions in how to chew gum, but here's an important piece of advice when using nicotine gum that you might not be aware of:

Don't just chew it!

I know myself that when I have a sweet in my mouth, I can't resist the temptation to crunch on it. With nicotine gum however, if you just keep chewing it, the nicotine will come out too quickly to be absorbed in the mouth; you will swallow it, and it will be wasted.

Nicotine from the gum has to be absorbed through the lining of the mouth to work. Nicotine that goes into the stomach is sent straight to the liver, where it is broken down before it can reach the brain.

So what you need to do is to chew the gum a couple of times, then 'park' it in the side of your mouth for ten seconds or more, then chew again and so on. That way you will get maximum value from the product. (This will also help you avoid getting hiccups, which is what happens when nicotine irritates the lining of the stomach.)

Here's another piece of advice: *don't wait until you are experiencing a craving to chew the gum.*

It takes about 15–20 minutes before enough nicotine gets into your system to make a difference – by that time it could be too late!

The best strategy is to decide to chew at least one piece each hour, regardless of how you are feeling – and more often when things are likely to be tough. In other words, make sure you have enough nicotine in your system to start with and anticipate when you are likely to need more.

And my final top piece of advice is: *don't just use the gum – combine it with the nicotine patch.*

There is now very good evidence that using the two together will give you the relief you need from cravings and withdrawal symptoms and make a big difference to become a permanent non-smoker.

I've noticed that I get very different reactions from people when they first try nicotine gum. Some people are fine with it, but others say that it tastes like cigarette ash or pepper. I think that the 'cigarette ash' idea is just because they are mixing up in their heads the chemical nicotine with cigarettes. But the smell (and, so people presume, the flavour) of cigarette ash comes from tens of thousands of chemicals, none of which is nicotine.

On the other hand, nicotine does taste peppery and some people find it hard to get used to. When people say it tastes disgusting I remind them that inhaling cigarette smoke takes some getting used to at first, but they seem to have managed it!

So if you are going to use nicotine gum my advice is:

- Try the 4-milligram gum first.
- Buy the cheapest one you can find that tastes okay.
- Don't chew continuously – chew a couple of times, then park it, then chew again, then park and so on.
- Make sure you chew at least ten pieces per day for at least six weeks.
- Use it with one of the forms of nicotine patch.

Nicotine skin patch

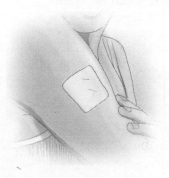

If they are not careful, people who work in tobacco fields quite often get symptoms of nicotine poisoning simply by brushing up continually against the tobacco leaves. Why? Because nicotine is quite readily absorbed through the skin.

This led a group of researchers in California to the idea of the nicotine skin patch: a plaster you put on the skin. Nicotine within the plaster is released slowly and absorbed into the body.

I remember being invited to an expert meeting by a drug company that was considering developing this product. We already knew that nicotine gum could help smokers to stop – the question was: would a nicotine skin patch work as well or better? My view was that it wouldn't work. I thought that the absorption would be too slow and the fact that there was no activity involved apart from putting the patch on in the morning would lessen its effectiveness.

I was completely wrong! The patch has been a huge success. It works just as well as the gum and is very popular because it is discreet and easy to use.

I think the fact that the patch works just as well as the gum tells us something very important about smoking: need for nicotine plays a crucial part, even when there is no activity involved. This is the 'nicotine hunger' I talked about in Chapter 1.

When it comes to choosing the dose of patch, I would start with the 'standard' dose:

- 15 milligrams for 16-hour patches that you take off at night
- 21 milligrams for 24-hour patches that you leave on at night

The scientist and the Swedish navy

Lighting up in a submarine is not a great idea. So back in the 1970s, the Swedish navy was looking for something that submariners could use instead of smoking. Ove Ferno, who was working for a small pharmaceutical company called AB Leo was asked to find a solution. He knew that what was needed was something that would replace the nicotine that the sailors were getting from their cigarettes. The obvious answer was a pill they could swallow.

But there was a problem. Nicotine is poisonous except in very small doses. Smokers typically get one milligram of nicotine from a cigarette and the body gets rid of it pretty quickly. Swallowing a bottle of nicotine tablets would make you very sick. What if someone were to get hold of a bottle of these pills and swallow them? The results would not be pleasant.

Ove came up with an ingenious solution – chewing gum. The nicotine would be bound into a chewable substance and released slowly as a result of chewing. In other words, the nicotine would only be released if the gum was chewed. No one would eat a whole packet of gum – they couldn't. And, even if they did, the nicotine would mostly stay in the gum and not get into the bloodstream. Ingenious! And so was born nicotine chewing gum.

This became the first medical treatment in the western world designed to help smokers to stop, and led to the nicotine patch, nasal spray, various lozenges, an inhalator, a mouth spray and even the electronic cigarette. I say the western world, because in fact the gum was not the first medical treatment to help smokers to give up – the Russians had already found one 20 years earlier. But that is another story, which I will come to later (see page 161).

There's no point in starting with a lower dose, because it almost certainly it won't be enough.

The 24-hour patch was developed for people who need a cigarette first thing in the morning. Nicotine in the patch takes a few hours to get into your system, so by having it on all night you make sure you're covered as soon as you wake up.

There isn't good evidence that the 24-hour patches give better results than the 16-hour patches, so which one you choose is up to you. In any case you can always take the 24-hour patch off at night. And, in practice, it is quite rare for relapse to occur early in the morning so it probably doesn't matter than much.

Some of the patch manufacturers tell you that you should 'step down' your dose as you get to the end of the course – moving to lower-dose patches. The evidence on this is clear: it doesn't make any difference. By all means step down your dose if you want to, but you don't have to.

There are higher-dose patches available (25 milligrams), and if you are using the standard patch and another nicotine product and still experience nicotine-withdrawal symptoms and strong cravings, I would be inclined to try the higher dose patch.

There is quite good evidence that you get better results with the patch if you put it on a couple of weeks before you stop smoking. The reason for this, I think, is that the nicotine from the patch prevents a lot of the nicotine from your cigarettes reaching its target, so your brain gradually starts to lose interest in smoking because it is not getting as much out of it.

So here are some top tips for using the patch:

- Don't start with a low-dose patch – use the standard dose or a high dose.
- Use it with a faster acting nicotine product such as gum or spray.
- If you are not going to quit straight away, start using it a couple of weeks before you quit.

Nicotine nasal spray

I think that if you are really struggling to come off cigarettes, it is well worth giving the nasal spray a go. It is the fastest acting of the licensed nicotine products.

It's not to everyone's taste – it is quite an irritant to the nose at first. But it does give you a good nicotine hit. You'll notice the effects within a few minutes.

You might wonder why on earth you should put nicotine into your nose. Well, the idea is based on the kind of snuff that people used to take a couple of hundred years ago. (You might have seen this in films – where some 'dandy' takes out his silver snuff box, opens it up, takes a pinch of snuff from it and sniffs it into his nose. He then sneezes and wipes his nose with his lace handkerchief.)

Snuff is just powdered tobacco mixed with flavourings, and the reason it was so popular is that it is a very efficient way of getting nicotine into the bloodstream. That is because the nose has what is called a 'leaky membrane' and is very well supplied with blood – as anyone who suffers from nose bleeds will testify! This means that anything you stick up your nose will have a very rapid route into your bloodstream.

Even as you read this, you are probably thinking about other drugs that are sniffed such as cocaine – the same idea applies.

The nicotine nasal spray is basically just a bottle of nicotine solution with a device like a perfume sprayer on the top so that when you press it, it gives a mist of nicotine spray. You stick it in your nose and spray once into each nostril.

Personally, I think the nasal spray would be better if it were twice the strength, but if you need more you can always put two sprays in each nostril.

In case you are worried that you will end up damaging the membranes in your nose – don't fret. It's not like cocaine; there is no evidence that it has any harmful effect.

The only other thing I'll say about the nasal spray is that it is worth persevering with if you are finding that other nicotine products don't come up to the mark.

r e s e a r c h

Preference makes no difference!

I was involved in a study some years ago in which we compared the nasal spray, gum and patch. Before we started, we asked all the smokers which they would prefer. Then we took no notice of that and gave them one of the products purely at random. The most interesting finding was that even when our volunteers didn't get what they said they wanted, within a week or so they came to like the product they ended up with.

Nicotine lozenge

The idea of the lozenges is that you suck on them and they act rather like nicotine gum – releasing nicotine into the mouth, where it is absorbed. Just like the nicotine gum, you don't want the nicotine coming out too fast or you'll just end up swallowing it.

There are a few different types of nicotine lozenge, with different sizes, different flavours, and different amounts of nicotine. In my opinion, the NiQuitin mini lozenge is one of the best products of this type. It releases the nicotine quite quickly and, because it is small, you don't end up having to suck it for half an hour.

Inhaler (inhalator)

There is only one brand of inhaler on the market at the moment, and it is Nicorette. The most important thing to know about this product is that, despite the name, no nicotine gets into your lungs – it is all absorbed in the mouth and throat. This means that it takes just as long to get a useful dose as with the gum or lozenge.

The inhaler looks a bit like one of those cigarette holders you see in the old films except that, instead of having a cigarette on the end, it has a little cartridge containing a bit of sponge with nicotine in it. When you puff on it, you draw air over the sponge and the nicotine vapour comes along with it.

The thing about nicotine vapour is that unless it is attached to a small particle or droplet – for example the tar particle in tobacco smoke – it sticks to the lining of your mouth and never gets down into the lungs.

Some people like the inhaler because using it is a bit like smoking and it gives them something to do with their hands. The funny thing is that we have good evidence that *this makes absolutely no difference to your cravings*. We find that the nicotine patch, which could not give you less to do with your hands, is just as good at relieving your cravings as the inhaler.

Something that I don't fully understand about the inhaler is that a lot of smokers say that they find it quite harsh in the throat when they first try it. This is odd because, as smokers, they should have got quite used to inhaling smoke, so why would they find nicotine vapour more irritating?

Perhaps the answer is that cigarette smoke is actually easier to inhale than pure nicotine. When the nicotine is attached to the tar particle it gets coated in a nice friendly mixture of chemicals that soften the nicotine irritancy. It's just a pity that those chemicals are the ones that cause lung cancer…

My main advice if you are going to use the inhaler is:

- Use it more often than it says in the instructions – it actually doesn't give you very much nicotine.
- Keep the tip warm when you are puffing on it – for example, by keeping your hand over it; this will improve the amount of nicotine you can get from it.
- Use the patch as well.
- Use it at least every hour, and more often if you need to.

Nicotine mouth spray

You may find the idea of a nicotine mouth spray a bit odd. It was the invention of one of the world's top experts on smoking, Professor Karl Fagerström, based in Sweden.

The principle is similar to the gum and lozenges: nicotine is absorbed through the lining of the mouth. The rate of absorption is not as fast as the nasal spray but obviously much faster than the patch.

There is much less research on the mouth spray than on the other nicotine products, but if this kind of thing appeals to you, then by all means try it. One thing to think about is that it is a bit more expensive than other products.

From what smokers tell me, it is something you tend to like or hate. Some people really don't like the taste, while others find it perfectly fine.

If you are going to use the mouth spray – apart from the usual advice of making sure you use it regularly and for at least six weeks, and using it with the patch – the only other thing I would say is to try out different techniques for getting the spray into the cheeks – it's good to experiment to find a way of doing it efficiently.

Nicotine oral film

This is a thin strip that dissolves completely in the mouth, releasing nicotine as it does so. Just like the gum and lozenge, the nicotine is absorbed through the lining of the mouth. Its selling points are that it is less expensive than the lozenges and dissolves quickly.

I can't tell you any more than that because it is very new – but it could be worth a try.

Now you've got some basic information about the available nicotine products, let's drill down a little more on some key points.

How much nicotine do you get from these products?

You might see from your cigarette pack that each cigarette gives about one milligram of nicotine and then look at, say, your nicotine gum pack and see that the gum has about four milligrams of nicotine in it. If I didn't know better, that would worry me; surely it can't be safe to get four times as much nicotine from the gum as from a cigarette?

Don't worry. Your brain does not actually receive four milligrams of nicotine – four milligrams is what the gum *contains*, but a lot of it is never released and much of the rest you swallow so it never reaches your brain. And because the nicotine is released slowly, you never see the nicotine spikes you see with cigarettes. So the effective dose you get from nicotine products is typically quite a bit lower than from smoking – regardless of what it says on the packet.

Fear of being poisoned by nicotine is one of the main reasons that smokers do not use their nicotine products properly. That's understandable because it's not just smokers who are concerned – even the so-called experts at the US Food and Drug Administration are being overcautious and giving what I think is unhelpful advice to smokers. This shouldn't make a difference to British smokers, but I mention it because, quite reasonably, some people will look at the US warnings and be worried. But there's no need. The American regulators just haven't caught up with the science yet (but they're getting there ...).

As I have mentioned already, the evidence now tells us that the best way to use the nicotine products is to use a skin patch *plus* one of the faster acting products such as the gum. The evidence also tells us that even if smokers are not ready to quit completely, they can use one of the nicotine products to help them cut down, because that will increase their chances of quitting later.

Using a nicotine product to cut down on smoking

Using nicotine replacements to help cut down on cigarettes before you quit can be effective. But many smokers are wary and it's no surprise why – those US regulators advise against it and make the companies put dire warnings on the nicotine packets to frighten consumers into limiting how much of the product they use and how long they use it for. Here's why you shouldn't be put off:

The average smoker takes in about 20 milligrams of nicotine per day and the liver disposes of it very quickly. At this dose it poses no significant health risk for the vast majority of people. Nicotine products typically give a lot less than this; the dire warnings are unfounded. Even if smokers do end up taking in too much they will just start to feel sick and will naturally reduce their dose long before they come to any harm. What's more, people who smoke and use nicotine products at the same time unconsciously tend to reduce the amount they take in from their cigarettes to compensate.

In fact, in recognition of everything I've been telling you, the main expert advisory body to the NHS, known as NICE (the National Institute for Health and Care Excellence), has just recommended that all smokers start taking nicotine replacements, even if it's just to cut down.

The 'very good' author

Some years ago I received a call from the agent of a famous author. He had heard that I was an expert and was desperate for some advice. His author was trying to stop smoking but this had caused writer's block and the deadline was rapidly approaching on his new novel. Now, research that I and others have done shows very clearly that when smokers try to stop they find it harder to concentrate. Loss of concentration is a classic 'nicotine-withdrawal symptom' and can last for up to four weeks. For many of us, this is no big deal. But for an author, journalist or air traffic controller this is a *very* big deal.

Research also shows that the problem is quite easily solved by using one of the nicotine products. So naturally I advised the agent to tell his author to do that. 'He is already using nicotine gum,' came the reply. Hmm. That was odd. 'How much is he using?' I asked. 'Oh he's being *very good* and is keeping it to one piece a day'.

I hope by now you can see what he was doing wrong. Each piece of gum gives about the same amount of nicotine as one half of a cigarette. It would be like smoking a half of a cigarette a day. There's no way on earth that one piece of gum was going to help anything. Smokers are recommended to take at least ten pieces each day – minimum. I passed this on to the agent. The book was finished on time. I believe it sold very well.

Throughout this book I will return to the idea that it is vital for smokers to use enough of their medicine if they really want to set themselves free.

Ingredient 11: Electronic cigarette

Rating: ★ ★

What to say about electronic cigarettes? Are they a curse or a blessing? Time will tell. Certainly they arouse a lot of passionate debate among the people I work with. The idea behind electronic cigarettes is that they can provide a nearly safe way of 'smoking' in which you can continue to get your nicotine fix but without the nasty tar and toxic gases produced when tobacco is burned.

There are currently two RCTs on electronic cigarettes showing that they can help you stop (have a look at <http://www.smokefreeformula.com> for updates). Because they are so variable in how much nicotine they give you and the quality of manufacture, I can't give you a global view about their likely value as one of your ingredients.

But from what I know about nicotine and other nicotine products, I would expect those electronic cigarettes that give you a good amount of nicotine and are pleasant to use to be effective. Because of the variability I give them a two rather than a three star rating.

What are electronic cigarettes?

On 5 July 2012 a major incident occurred on a British motorway. A coach driver stopped his coach because some kind of vapour was seen emerging from one of the passenger's bags. Firefighters, armed police and bomb-disposal experts were called to the scene and surrounded the coach. The M6 was closed in both directions. All 48 passengers were evacuated and told by the police to keep their hands where they could see them. They were detained in rows under close guard while officers searched the coach. After a number of hours, the truth emerged. What had brought the M6 to a complete standstill? Was it a bomb? A terrorist attack? No. The suspicious object was revealed to be … an electronic cigarette!

Perhaps it is not surprising that police were unfamiliar with electronic cigarettes (or e-cigarettes) in 2012 – as they were very new, and still are. But their popularity has burgeoned over the last few years and in Britain there are now 1.3 million people using them. Most of those people are using them as well as smoking, to help them cut down on the amount that they smoke. But a quarter of all quit attempts now involve their use.

E-cigarettes deliver nicotine to the smoker rather like other nicotine products. The crucial thing is that they don't give the smoker tar or carbon monoxide – the chemicals in tobacco cigarettes that do the damage.

When you suck on an e-cigarette, a battery-powered heating element comes on. This warms up a nicotine plug, which releases nicotine vapour. You then inhale this into the lungs, just like puffing on a tobacco cigarette. E-cigarettes also have either glycerol or propylene glycol in them, to make it look as though you're breathing out smoke. In fact these chemicals are not smoke and are, as far as anyone has been able to tell, safe. They're just what is used for stage smoke in rock concerts and plays. Sometimes the manufacturers add a slight flavour to the smoke, but otherwise it has no odour apart from that of nicotine.

Danny – 42 years old – *stopped by using professional support*
Danny originally came from Ireland but now lives in London. He works in security and is married with no children.

I started smoking when I was 12. The usual thing, just peer pressure and all that. I became 'needy' for them by the age of 15 and was buying them regularly. Me and my best friend would get 20 between us each week. They were pretty cheap then back in Ireland. And we dragged them out over the course of the week.

Danny's story about starting is 'textbook': starting because friends are smoking and quite quickly becoming 'needy' for them (I love that phrase).

As soon as I'd started smoking, I was always trying to stop. Even though my father and mother both smoked they were very anti-smoking and I was paranoid about smelling when I came in the house. I was also embarrassed about coughing.

Quickly realising the mistake in starting is common. Parental disapproval is important in deterring smoking in young people even if the parents themselves smoke.

I wanted to stop, but another part of me didn't. I knew it was really bad for me; after all there were warnings on packets. I would usually last a few days, but when the weekend came round somebody would offer me a cigarette.

Remember me talking about conflicting desires – the rider and the horse?

I finally stopped two years ago tomorrow. It was 15th May. I stopped with my wife; we both stopped the exact same day.

Danny stopped with a family member (Ingredient 18), which can be supportive. A lot of ex-smokers can remember the exact date they stopped – you could be one of them.

We went to the NHS Stop Smoking Service and saw a nurse in the local surgery. She monitored our progress and gave us support.

Evidence tells us that having a supportive professional involved can be very helpful (Ingredient 4).

The NHS service was a leg up. It was only ten minutes a week but it was good. We'd go there and blow into a machine. We didn't want to let the nurse down; she was gunning for us, so we didn't want to have to go there and tell her that we slipped.

The 'machine' is a carbon monoxide breathalyser which can tell whether you have smoked or not so you can't cheat. Knowing that you are accountable can be very motivating.

I used nicotine patches. I didn't need to have the massively strong ones because I never smoked at night and I never went over 20 a day.

Nicotine patches (Ingredient 10) reduce the cravings by dealing with the nicotine hunger.

During the first four weeks I didn't drink. I had a gig to go to on the Southbank on the first weekend after we'd stopped. I was going to see one of my favourite Irish folk bands. It was a big social event – they only come around every couple of years. I knew if I drank I wouldn't last. And I didn't drink.

Danny has shown great self-knowledge in avoiding alcohol (Ingredient 21), and this could have made all the difference.

I could never see myself going back to smoking. I've been like that for ages – since before I hit the one-year mark I just knew it.

After two years the chances of ever going back to smoking are very small, but vigilance is still required to avoid a silly slip up.

I love being a non-smoker. I've become a bit of a preacher about it to the lads at work. When I think about times back in Ireland when I used to smoke near my brother, who's a non-smoker, it makes me feel really bad.

Danny now identifies himself as a non-smoker (Ingredient 2). This is one of the best protections against going back.

There was nobody complaining louder than me when the smoking ban came in. I thought it was a disgrace, but now I think it's brilliant. When you do give up, you realise how anti-social you were towards people.

My research shows that the smoking ban has actually helped a lot of smokers to stop.

The single most important piece of advice I would give to someone trying to stop smoking is to get off to a good running start. Don't put yourself in a position where you're likely to be tempted. Once you're over the first week, you can tell yourself, 'Well, I haven't smoked in a week,' and a week becomes a month, and a month becomes six months, and six months becomes a year.

Lots of good advice here: most important is to get off to a good start and then to build on what you have achieved.

E-cigarettes mostly allow you to absorb nicotine more slowly than a cigarette (where you get a hit with every puff). The reason is that, although you're inhaling the vapour, most of it doesn't get into the lungs. Most of the vapour gets into the mouth and the upper airways, which don't have a big enough surface area for you to get that rapid absorption. It's more like nicotine gum or the lozenge.

The important thing to remember is that you're getting the nicotine into your system in a safe way. The nicotine itself doesn't cause damage. In fact the users don't call using an e-cigarette 'smoking'; the e-cigarette websites seems to prefer the term 'vaping' because of course there is no real smoke involved.

Unless there's a manufacturing fault or something wrong with the e-cigarette, it should be near enough safe. In theory, you can overdose on an e-cigarette, however by the time you got to that point you would know you were overdosing and start to feel sick. In practice, most of the e-cigarettes at the moment don't deliver anything like as much nicotine as a tobacco cigarette.

There are many different models and types of e-cigarettes out there. Some single e-cigarettes are disposable; others are refillable. By far the most popular e-cigarette in Britain at the moment is called Elites. That doesn't mean it is the best though. My advice would be to try different ones and see if you can find one you particularly get on with.

With reusable e-cigarettes you buy e-cigarette nicotine liquid and top up the little reservoir inside and recharge the battery. The initial cost of the refillable e-cigarettes is quite a lot, but it quickly becomes a lot cheaper than smoking normal cigarettes. At the time I am writing this, using e-cigarettes generally costs about half as much as smoking real ones.

The electronic-cigarette community

On the internet there's a large and growing community of e-cigarette users who are very passionate about them. Experienced users chat online and talk about how to get more nicotine out of e-cigarettes.

Here's one example of a tip: if you just puff on an e-cigarette like an ordinary cigarette, the moment you start puffing it heats up the element that starts to get the nicotine drawn off. However, it takes a while for the element to heat up. So by the time you've finished the puff you've not got much nicotine from it. What you can do in order to get more nicotine is to do a couple of quick puffs to heat up the element and then take a big draw. That gives you a better nicotine dose; that's something the users have learned themselves.

Do electronic cigarettes work?

Perhaps the biggest question is: do e-cigarettes help people stop smoking? At the moment we don't have a lot of direct evidence on them. We know they can deliver nicotine, and can help with the craving and withdrawal symptoms. And we also know that there's a big community of people out there who swear by them, and really like them.

At the moment most people in that community are using them to cut down the amount of cigarettes they smoke, but they're hoping to stop eventually. Some people use them like other nicotine products: they stop smoking real cigarettes and start using e-cigarettes. Our figures show that people who are usually 20-a-day smokers don't smoke fewer cigarettes while they're on e-cigarettes. But we think they're taking in less nicotine from the conventional cigarettes as a result of using them. So they're not using e-cigarettes to take in even more nicotine; they're not puffing as hard on their usual cigarettes. This has the bonus that they take in less tar and carbon monoxide.

There's a very good book that's just been written by my colleague, Professor Jean-François Etter. It is simply called *The Electronic Cigarette: An Alternative to Tobacco?* It's worth a read.

Electronic cigarettes and smoking indoors

One of the things advertisers of e-cigarettes talk about is that you can smoke them inside. Legally, that is correct because they don't produce smoke. There's no health reason to ban them because they're not dangerous and they don't stink out the place like real cigarettes. However, because of the confusion that exists between e-cigarettes and real cigarettes, there are some places that will ban you from using them. I'm conflicted about this. On the one hand, there is no particular reason to ban them on health grounds, but on the other, it would feel like a backward step to see people doing something akin to smoking indoors.

As e-cigarettes start to become more popular and well known that sort of confusion will fade away, and you'll probably be able to use them in more places. Even on a coach on the M6 …

Some countries have banned electronic cigarettes

Oddly, some countries – including Canada and Australia – have near-enough banned e-cigarettes. Perhaps the governments think that because it has the word 'cigarette' in it, it has to be bad for you. On the other hand, they haven't actually banned real cigarettes.

I suppose the thinking is that the governments don't want any more nicotine products on the market for people to get addicted to. I think this is wrong: right now in Britain there's hardly anyone using e-cigarettes who isn't (or wasn't until recently) a smoker. One of the concerns is that children might start using e-cigarettes and then move on to real cigarettes. But in my opinion that isn't very likely to happen. Nicotine products don't tend to be 'gateway drugs' that lead non-smokers into smoking. They don't quite have the dangerous qualities of real cigarettes so they don't have that rebellious aura that attracts so many teenagers to smoking but I may be wrong ...

To recap, my key messages for e-cigarettes are:

- They are almost certainly safe, but with so many brands on the market and very little testing, I would stick to the major brands.
- There's a strong consumer base out there of people who love them, and find them an acceptable alternative to smoking.
- There's a thriving online community where users discuss methods of using them better and which ones to use.
- They're evolving all the time, so you should keep a look out for new models because they're improving a lot.
- There is no reason yet to think that they are better than licensed nicotine products, but if you have tried those other products and think that e-cigarettes might be more suited to you, by all means give them a go.

Chapter 11

Stop-smoking Medicines

The previous chapter covered different types of nicotine product that you could use to help reduce your urges to smoke. This chapter looks at pills containing things other than nicotine that can achieve the same aim.

If you don't think it seems right to take a medicine to help you stop smoking, I completely understand. All medicines have side effects. Also, there is something about stopping smoking that seems like you should be able to do it without a chemical crutch. Millions of people manage to stop without taking medicines. In any case, no magic pill is going to take away your desire to smoke – only you can do that.

What's more, you might have a perfectly reasonable distrust of drug companies. They have not covered themselves in glory over the years – as scandal after scandal reveals that they have been willing to hide and distort evidence to keep people using drugs that might be harming them, or at least not doing them any good. I feel the same way, even though I occasionally do consultancy work for some of the companies that are marketing stop-smoking medicines (and nicotine products).

I look at it like this. Suppose you discover that you have cancer of the throat. If you catch this early it can be cured by a combination of radiotherapy and drugs. I hope you wouldn't think twice about using these treatments, as there is a good chance that they would save your life.

Drug companies and me

In the 30 odd years I have been working with drug companies to help them develop and test their products to help smokers to stop, I've met some really nice people who care about what they do and work incredibly hard, and I've noticed something very interesting: they get really fired up by working on stop-smoking medicines, because finally they are working on something that can really make a difference to people's lives.

Having said that, I'm not so naive as to believe that drug companies only have your interests at heart. Their boards of directors are charged with maximising the profits to shareholders and there are plenty of documented cases of unethical practices that mean that people in my position have to be very wary not to get caught up in their agenda when this conflicts with public health.

So – when drug companies want to develop better products or conduct rigorous evaluations of their products, people like me have a role to play. When they want to 'big up' their products or get an edge over their competitors – they're on their own.

What's the difference? Using a drug to help you stop smoking or using a drug to cure a disease caused by smoking? As it happens the drugs to help you stop have very limited side effects and are very cheap, while the drugs to cure the smoking-related diseases are expensive and unpleasant to take.

To me, it would purely be a question of what would help me to achieve my goal. If I have a bad headache, I take aspirin or paracetamol. I don't think of myself as a wimp for doing this.

I truly want you to have the best chance of stopping for good every single time you try. I'll be happy when *The SmokeFree Formula* becomes a museum piece that people will look at in a glass case and wonder what on earth the human species was thinking when so many of its members were smoking! So, do please give serious consideration to using one of the stop-smoking medicines that are available. I'm recommending them because they help a lot of people.

One thing to remember is that it is safe to use these medicines with nicotine products described in the previous chapter, although the evidence we have at the moment has not shown any clear benefit from doing that.

Ingredient 12: Varenicline (Champix)

Rating: ★ ★ ★

This is a pill you typically take for 12 weeks, starting a week or so before your quit date – though you can take it for longer. You will need a prescription from your doctor.

There are loads of RCTs showing that it is very effective in helping you achieve lasting success.

Despite some claims in the press, it is safe, but it can make you feel sick and keep you awake at night. It is not recommended for use during pregnancy.

I vividly remember when I first saw the results of tests of this drug. A contact at the drug company, Pfizer, got in touch and told me that she wanted to come and share with me the findings from two RCTs they had carried out. They had been quite bold and carried out two nearly identical studies comparing varenicline with a drug called bupropion (see below, Ingredient 13) and a placebo.

I guessed they were quite confident that their drug would be at least as good as bupropion, which had been getting good results for a few years – but I'd seen drug company confidence before. I remember in the 1990s doing a clinical trial for Glaxo Wellcome (now GlaxoSmithKline) who were convinced that their drug, ondansetron, would help smokers to stop. I told them before the trial that it didn't seem very likely to me because the effect it had on the brain was all wrong. But they wanted to go ahead and I agreed to run the study. When we finished the study, but before we knew who had got the drug and who had got a placebo, I actually thought it might have worked, as the overall quitting success rates were remarkably good. Alas, when it came to 'unblinding' – finding out who had been given the active drug and who had got placebo – there was no difference at all between the two groups. Frankly, even though this was what I had predicted, I was disappointed. So what had led to the high success rate? I can only put it down to my colleague Peter Hajek's very effective group treatment programme, in which the active drug group and the placebo group had both taken part.

Anyway, I had learned to be sceptical when drug companies were excited about their results, so when I got the call to look at the data Pfizer had, I was interested but not expecting too much. I asked my colleague Professor Martin Jarvis to be in the meeting because he is someone whose judgement I trust and I thought it would be good to have another person there to act as a reference point.

I'm glad I did. When they showed us the graphs of the numbers of volunteer smokers who had stopped for at least a year and been given either varenicline, bupropion or placebo, the results were very striking. Both drugs did better than the placebo, but varenicline did almost twice as well as bupropion – in both the studies.

I had not seen anything like it. The result could not have been clearer. Taking varenicline was much more effective at helping these smokers to stop than taking bupropion – and bupropion was better than placebo. Martin and I looked at each other, as though for reassurance that what we were seeing was real. If these results were to be believed, this was a major breakthrough. Here was a pill that was considerably better than anything we currently had available.

Since then, there have been more than a dozen studies showing this drug to be very effective in helping smokers to stop. It is definitely more effective overall than bupropion and probably somewhat more effective for a lot of smokers than using nicotine products.

The drug works by beating nicotine at its own game. I explained in Chapter 1 how nicotine hijacks the reward pathway in our brain by attaching itself to receptor cells. Varenicline binds to these receptors first, blocking nicotine from doing its work, and then stops your animal brain screaming for more cigarettes.

If I were stopping smoking now, I think this is the drug I would try first.

Side effects and scare stories

There has been a lot in the press over the past few years about varenicline. You might have read wild tales of it causing people to commit suicide or behave aggressively and even claims that it causes heart problems.

Let's look at the facts. The trouble first started when a local paper in the US reported a story of a musician who got drunk and went round to his neighbour to shout at him through the door. His neighbour shot him dead. What has this got to do with varenicline, you might ask? Well, it turns out that the man who was shot (yes, that's right – the man who was shot, not the man who did the shooting) was taking varenicline to help him stop smoking. Somehow or other the press managed to make out that varenicline was responsible for all this. You may think this is bonkers – and it is – but this sparked off a deluge of reported incidents, prompted, in my opinion, in some cases by lawyers out to make a fast buck. The media stories fuelled these reports and they seemed to be settling into a pattern of people on varenicline being at greater risk of committing suicide.

You might be thinking that suicide is pretty serious and we should be worried about any kind of pattern. So what's going on? When a drug is being taken by several million people, you're always going to find that bad things have happened to some of them. Because, alas, bad things happen all the time. Someone, somewhere in the world, has just had a heart attack right after taking an aspirin. I can say that because so many millions of people take aspirin that it's bound to happen purely by chance. The only way to know whether the drug played any part in this is to look at whether the rate is any higher than among similar kinds of people who are not taking it.

There have now been two very large studies comparing smokers taking varenicline with smokers taking other stop-smoking medicines or nicotine products and these found no difference in the rate at which people committed suicide. What's more, there are now plenty of studies clearly showing that smokers who use varenicline to help them stop suffer *less* from mood disturbance caused by nicotine withdrawal, including feeling depressed, than those who use a placebo.

The most recent scare with varenicline was that it caused heart problems. I won't go into the details but, again, when others have repeated the study properly no significant increased risk could be found. There is still research going on to find out more, but at the moment the medicine regulators in the UK don't think that varenicline will give you heart trouble.

Of course none of this stops lawyers going after Pfizer for compensation claims in the US. Elsewhere in the world, claims of side effects are much rarer.

Now, of course we all have to watch out for side effects, and no drugs are completely without them. In the case of varenicline the ones that have been found to come from taking the drug are feeling sick and difficulty sleeping. In both cases the large majority of users are so pleased not to be experiencing cigarette cravings, perhaps for the first time ever, that they are more than happy to put up with them.

So if your doctor says you can't have varenicline because it is dangerous, just point them to the website of the 'Medicines and Healthcare Regulatory Agency' – which they should be familiar with. This is the organisation that says whether drug companies can market their drugs in the UK. It bases its judgements on whether there is good evidence that the drugs are truly beneficial and whether any side effects outweigh those benefits.

How long to take varenicline for

The standard course for varenicline is 12 weeks – and you usually start taking the medicine a week before your target quit date. One large study showed that you can get better long-term success if you keep taking the drug for 24 weeks, but this extended period of use only seems to be necessary if you didn't manage to stop on your target quit date but carried on smoking for a bit longer.

My advice is that if you stopped smoking a week after starting the drug and haven't smoked for the other 11 weeks, you probably don't need to continue taking it after that. But if you struggled at first and didn't manage to stop until a few weeks after the date you had set yourself, it would be a good idea to keep taking the drug for a further 12 weeks.

This is all explained on the label in the packet, but the chances are your doctor won't know this. In that case, you might want to suggest, very nicely, they read the label.

Ingredient 13: Bupropion (Zyban)

Rating: ★ ★ ★

Bupropion is a pill that helps you stop smoking by reducing the urges to smoke and making smoking a little less rewarding to the animal part of your brain. There are lots of RCTs which show that it can help achieve lasting success. Also real world studies in the English Stop Smoking Services confirm that it is effective.

It is not as effective in general as varenicline or using what we call 'dual form' nicotine replacement therapy (see Ingredients 10 and 11), but if you have tried those and they didn't work for you, it might give you another route to quitting.

You will need a prescription. You shouldn't use it if you have any kind of tendency to seizure (having fits) or if you suffer from anorexia or bulimia. The main side effect is disturbed sleep, but very occasionally people get an allergic reaction. Again, this drug is not recommended for use in pregnancy.

Bupropion (called Zyban when used to help you stop smoking and Wellbutrin when used in the US as an anti-depressant) is a very mild stimulant. Its effect in helping smokers to stop was discovered by accident when a doctor, Professor Linda Ferry, heard from colleagues about a pattern in which smokers who were given the drug for depression seemed to go off smoking.

The drug has now been thoroughly researched and is widely used in many countries around the world. It was subject to the same scare stories as varenicline but in this case, because it is a mild stimulant, there are cases, extremely rare, of smokers having seizures. This would not be expected unless you are already at some risk, for example because of a head injury.

Bupropion is much cheaper than varenicline and it can be effective so it is worth trying. However, in general it is not as effective.

Because bupropion also works as an anti-depressant you may want to consider it if you have a tendency towards depression. Having said that, the evidence I've seen doesn't lead me to think it is better at tackling the mood problems that can occur when you stop smoking than varenicline.

Stop-smoking drugs and your doctor

The slight disadvantage of varenicline and bupropion is that you have to get a prescription from your doctor. In my experience very few doctors know enough about stop-smoking medicines. This isn't their fault; there are so many different drugs for different conditions that they can't be an expert in everything. What it means, however, is that you might have to be the expert! After all, stopping smoking means more to you than it does to them.

I have armed you with what I think are the main pieces of information. If your doctor doesn't believe you (or me), then just point him or her to the following websites, which will back up everything you and I are saying:

- <http://www.mhra.gov.uk> – the website of the UK medicine regulatory body
- <http://www.thecochranelibrary.com> – the website of the most important scientific studies
- <http://www.nice.org.uk> – the website of NICE: the organisation in Britain that provides guidance to doctors on what they are supposed to be doing

Combining buproprion and nicotine products

A large study in the US found that using bupropion and a nicotine product together gave better results than using either alone, but other studies since then have failed to find any benefit. So there isn't good evidence, but if you're using bupropion and still struggling with urges, adding nicotine products is something you might want to consider.

Ingredient 14: Cytisine (Tabex)

Rating: ★ ★ ★

Cytisine is a pill that helps you stop smoking in a similar way to varenicline. In countries such as Russia and Poland you can just buy it from a shop – you don't need a prescription. In other countries in Central and Eastern Europe you have to get a prescription from a doctor. In the UK and the rest of the world, it is not licensed yet.

However this situation could change fairly soon, as more evidence becomes available. In theory you might be able to get a doctor to prescribe it, or you could buy some on the Internet; however I would advise against buying medicine online – you don't know what you are getting and there is no comeback if you are sold something else that could harm you.

In my view, the sooner cytisine is licensed across the world the better. This is not because I think it is better than, say, varenicline – it is because it is much cheaper (or should be). It can be made so cheaply that just about anyone in the world could afford it.

It has been found to be safe to use, though use in pregnancy is not advised. The main side effect is stomach upset, but this is usually quite mild.

I mentioned in the previous chapter that long before the Western world started making products to help smokers stop Russia had already done research of its own.

During the Second World War many soldiers used to smoke what they called 'false tobacco'. This was leaves from a plant called Cytisus Laburnum, known to us simply as laburnum. They found from their own experience that it helped with their tobacco cravings when they couldn't get cigarettes. The Russians followed up on this and, as early as the 1960s, began doing studies on whether an extract from laburnum seeds called cytisine would help smokers to stop.

The results proved positive and a Bulgarian company called Sopharma has been making the drug ever since. It is widely available in former Communist bloc countries (Russia, Poland, Hungary, etc.) as a tablet called Tabex. By the time you read this, it may be licensed in a number of other countries. It may be a little longer before it is licensed in the UK and western Europe. We are little behind the game!

The current licence for Tabex involves you taking it for just four weeks – starting a week before your target quit date and continuing for three weeks afterwards. You start by taking six of the little pills each day and gradually work your way down to one. (Taking six pills may seem like a lot, but the pills are very small.) No one seems to know why this particular way of taking the drug developed, but my guess is that it comes from the fact that the drug is not very well transported from the blood into the brain so you have to start with quite a large dose to have the desired effect.

The only side effect of this drug that we have been able to discover is an upset stomach, and this is normally mild. In the study we did on the drug, no one found the stomach upset so bad that they stopped taking the drug.

More than 4 million people have taken the drug in Europe without any sign of serious side effects. As I've said before, no drug can be considered completely safe but this one looks as safe as any.

I hope that it will be granted a marketing licence in the UK soon. It is so cheap it could save the NHS tens of millions of pounds, which it badly needs.

Rob – 45 years old – *stopped after his father died of lung disease*
Rob works as a stop-smoking advisor.

I started smoking at 24 because I had a friend who smoked these French cigarettes, and I liked the smell of them. I thought they were slightly different – it wasn't really like smoking. I could never see myself smoking something as vulgar as a Silk Cut.

Identity plays a role not just in whether you smoke, but what kind of cigarette you go for.

Ridiculously I can still remember the first time I bought a pack of cigarettes. I got a bit embarrassed because I was smoking my friend's cigarettes so I thought I'd buy a pack and give him them back. And after about six to nine months I moved on from black tobacco.

Peer pressure doesn't have to involve someone actively trying to get you to smoke – in most cases it is just that people in your social world are doing it.

I wasn't really happy being a smoker; every cigarette was a fresh episode of ambivalence. I was never a dependent, wake-up-and-have-one-in-the-morning-type smoker – I smoked when I socialised. But I socialised a lot.

A good example of how even situational smoking can be very addictive.

I remember when I was a child my mother was always trying to quit. She'd maybe do three or four days and then go back to smoking. She died at 55 of cancer of the pancreas.

Cancer of the pancreas is a smoking-related disease.

I finally quit after possibly a couple of hundred half-hearted attempts. I was in my mid to late thirties. I'd had a child a couple of years before and I didn't want my son to see me smoking. Then my father died of COPD. I have asthma and that was a real wake up call; my father's death made me realise that for me it was not a question of 'whether' smoking would kill me but 'when'.

Different reasons for doing things stack up. Not wanting Rob's son to see him smoking was not enough on its own, but it created the 'tension' – and his father's death was the 'trigger' that finally did the trick.

When I was giving up and we had a party at our house, there were lots of people smoking and I got a cigarette off someone else and thought I'd smoke it later. But when it came to it, there wasn't really anywhere I could smoke it.

Even the most determined quit attempt can be derailed by being with other smokers.

I stopped without support but I would advise anyone who has tried to stop before and gone back to smoking to see a stop-smoking advisor and use one of the stop-smoking medicines. If they had been available back in the 1970s I think my parents might still be alive.

Rob is one of Britain's top stop-smoking advisors and he knows what he is talking about.

Chapter 12

Staying Strong

You can think of stopping smoking as a campaign and each attempt as a battle – a fight to the death. You are like a warrior in the Middle Ages. What is going to help you win the battle?

The previous chapters have been about your armour – how you protect yourself from the urges to smoke – and how you can weaken your enemy through nicotine products and stop-smoking medicines. This chapter is about the tactics you can use to dodge the blows that cravings aim at you.

All you have to do to be a non-smoker is not to smoke ... but sometimes it can feel like trying to stop yourself breathing. The trouble is that your animal brain doesn't know the difference – and treats them both pretty much the same. (Although, to be fair, stopping yourself from breathing is actually harder than stopping yourself from smoking, which is just as well!)

So you will still need to stay strong. There are several strategies you can adopt for this. This chapter describes the ones that I think may be most useful.

It is much easier *not* to do something when you have something else to do instead. If you take something out of your life that has been as much a part of it as smoking, it is going to leave a big cigarette-shaped hole.

Ingredient 15: Plan things to keep busy

Rating: ★ ★

You will know yourself that distraction can be helpful in stopping you thinking about things you shouldn't. I don't know of any studies looking at this with smoking, but I think that you should plan some kind of distraction as one of the weapons in your armoury for when you feel the urge to smoke. You might also get a lot of things done that you have been meaning to do for ages!

Boredom, or simply having time on your hands, is bad news when you are trying to stop smoking. This is partly because you probably will have used cigarettes in the past to fill those gaps in the day when there is nothing much going on. Nicotine hitting your brain receptors kids you into thinking you're doing something constructive when you are not. Your animal brain can't tell the difference between nicotine reward and reward from a job well done. Either way, it is satisfied.

So, are there things you can plan to do to replace that satisfaction, that will occupy those moments when you would have smoked and give you a sense of accomplishment? A thorough spring clean of the house? A neglected hobby? A book you have been meaning to read? Sorting out your CD/vinyl collection? A computer game you have got stuck on? A box set of a TV show you have been meaning to watch? A puzzle book you were given for your birthday? A room that needs decorating?

If this is something you think that would work for you, then decide now what you will do. If you can't think of anything, then it could be worth talking it over with someone close to you for ideas.

Ingredient 16: Tell other people about stopping

Rating: ★

About half of smokers like to tell other people they are quitting so they can help – or at least not get in the way – and about half don't.

I can tell you with confidence that whichever of these you want to do is fine, but if you tell other people you are quitting it can at least get you used to being treated like a non-smoker.

You might read in some stop-smoking guides that you should tell other people you are stopping. You can see why this seems to make sense. But you may also feel that going public with your quit attempt is too open and could be embarrassing if you don't make it.

Of course you might have no choice about telling some people you are not smoking. Obviously if you live with a smoker, you are going to have to say something. Then there is the question of what exactly you tell them. Have a think about these options and see which one you feel comfortable with:

Whether or not you decide to tell people that you are trying to stop smoking, or have become a non-smoker or whatever, you are going to have to find a way to respond when people offer you a cigarette or ask if you are 'coming outside for a fag break'.

If being offered a cigarette or asked out for a fag break was what took you back to smoking before, I would advise you to have your response ready and well rehearsed this time. A few options are:

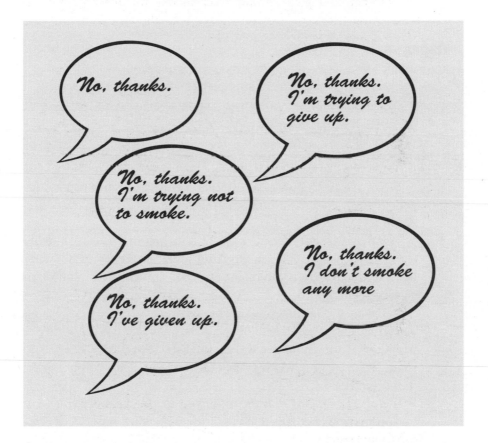

Have a think about which of these you feel most comfortable with. I don't have any evidence to help with this, but I suspect that one of these will feel more comfortable than the others.

One thing I would say is: don't be afraid to say that you've given up or that you don't smoke any more. It puts you under a bit more pressure not to go back to smoking, and it might invite scepticism, but that extra bit of motivation might be useful for you.

But remember too that what you tell other people and how you feel don't need to be the same thing at all. You can be totally committed inside to stopping but tell other people that you are 'trying to stop' just to avoid the kind of conversation you'd rather do without.

Ingredient 17: Count how much money is being saved

Rating: ★

You probably have quite a good idea how much you spend every week on cigarettes. Since the cost of smoking is an important reason for quitting for a lot of people, it makes sense to see how much you are saving every day that you don't smoke. It's amazing how quickly it adds up.

When you think how much smoking costs, and what you get for your money, it seems a little crazy! Almost no smokers think it is worth it.

You may well have found ways of reducing the cost of smoking – smoking cheaper brands, smoking fewer cigarettes or smoking hand-rolled cigarettes. You might even buy smuggled or counterfeit cigarettes or tobacco.

In Britain the average smoker spends more than £20 per week on cigarettes. I find it interesting that the amount spent is the same for people with very little money as smokers with plenty of cash to spare. Smokers on lower incomes pay less per cigarette but smoke more cigarettes.

It is also interesting that the more you spend, the more you want to stop smoking. Perhaps that is not too surprising, but it does reinforce the view that raising the cost of smoking is one of the most important things that governments can do to encourage and help smokers to stop.

Here are some ideas to help you count your savings:

1 Put the cash you would have spent every day in a jar and put the jar somewhere where you come across it regularly.

2 Use one of the free stop-smoking smartphone apps which asks you

how much you spend on cigarettes and then calculates how much you have saved as each day without cigarettes goes by. (I think SF28 – available from <http://www.sf28.co.uk> – is pretty good, but then I helped design it!)

3 Use one of the free stop-smoking websites that does pretty much the same thing.
4 Open a bank account and set up a direct debit into it.

If you are paying for nicotine products or a prescription charge for a stop-smoking medicine, obviously the gain will be that much less. But you will still save, and every penny counts, as they say.

Ingredient 18: Quit with friends or family

> ### Rating: ★
> There is a some evidence that quitting with a 'buddy' can help, so you may like to try this if you can find someone willing to quit with you. If you are going to do this, then there are a few things you can do to give it the best the chance of working.

A friend of mine who was a sheep farmer in Australia (and one of Australia's top smoking experts) told me that when sheep get separated from the rest of the flock – for example if they wander out of their field into a wood where they can't find their way back – they simply give up and die. I can believe it. Most of us are a bit like that too. We like to do things together and we get lonely when we don't have someone to share our experiences with.

Stopping smoking with a buddy seems like a sensible thing to do, but the evidence on whether it really helps or not is mixed.

My friend and colleague Dr Martin Edwards and I conducted an RCT many years ago in which one group of smokers from his practice was given advice each week from a nurse about stopping, using a method very similar to the one described in Ingredient 4 (seeing a professional stop-smoking advisor). The other group was exactly the same except that when the smokers first came to the surgery they were paired up. The person they were paired with was usually a complete stranger. At every visit they were always seen in pairs. And they were asked to phone each other every day for the first week to check how the other was getting along and support each other.

I know what you are thinking. Yes – having the support of a complete stranger might be an added incentive to stay off cigarettes, but on the other hand there is a risk that if one of the pair relapses they will drag the other person down with them. So our results could have gone either way.

What happened was that the buddy pairs did better than the people seen on their own. It wasn't a very big study and we only followed the volunteers up for the first few weeks so we don't know if the effect lasted. But it looked promising.

As far as I know, no one has tried to repeat this study, but we later did another study that was not very different involving stop-smoking groups. Half the groups followed the programme designed by Professor Peter Hajek, which included pairing up smokers in the group so that they could be 'stop-smoking buddies'. Like our first study, they were supposed to call each other every day. They also played Peter's 'betting game'. In this game, each pair agrees an amount of money to stake on whether they will make it through the next week. The twist is that if one member of the pair relapses, both of them lose the money.

This may seem unfair but you can probably see that this would be more motivating than just losing your own money if you relapse. Your partner would lose his or her stake if you didn't turn up the next week, or if you turned up and admitted you had smoked, or if you claimed you hadn't smoked but your CO reading was ten parts per million or more.

The amounts involved varied from less than £1 to £10. Money that was lost went into a kitty to be used for a small party for those who were left at the end of the course, four weeks after the target quit date.

What did we find? Nothing. No effect. Naturally we were disappointed. One explanation was we were just unlucky. Another is that we weren't skilled enough at getting the pairs to bond with each other and care enough about the other person to stay off cigarettes.

John – 66 years old – *stopped with his wife*

John works for an organisation that provides occupational health and safety advice to companies, unions and public sector organisations.

I started smoking when I was about ten. It was big because all the kids did it. It was what men did; and boys wanted to be men.

Wanting to be 'grown up' is an important factor in some people starting.

We lived on the streets in a very working-class area of Nottingham: Victorian terraced houses and streets. Smoking was just what you did. You could buy a fag and a match from the corner shop for a penny ha'penny. Usually Woodbine or Park Drive, the cheapest brands.

Notice the recurring theme of social norm and low cost.

I didn't think about giving up for a long time. The first ten years of my working life I was a coal miner. If I think back to those days there was absolutely no advice about smoking or not smoking. The coal board used to send mobile x-ray units around collieries once every three years, and that was to detect dust contamination of the lungs. But that was a health surveillance thing that was absolutely pointless in protecting people's health. All it did was to show how much dust you had inhaled and it didn't show on an X-ray until you were something like 20 per cent contaminated – which was too late.

I'm glad to say that we've come a long way in terms of caring for people in dangerous working environments, but even now a lot of workplaces tacitly support smoking, even though it is bad for business because of the number of sick days taken by smokers.

There was a tobacco company that used to come round and set up in the car park outside the canteen to promote smoking. You would go

The tobacco industry can't do this now in Britain obviously, but they have other ways of getting young people to smoke.

there, roll your own cigarette and stick it in this machine they had; if it drew a certain amount of strength from your cigarette, they gave you a free ounce of Golden Virginia tobacco and a packet of papers. They must have had the national coal board's permission to do that; the board didn't promote it themselves but they assisted those who did want to promote it. That was a fairly regular occurrence.

The first time I stopped I'd been having chest pains. I don't know if they were related to my smoking, but there was an element of fear in that.

Fear is a good spur to action – the trouble is that it is not so good at sustaining the change.

I then gave up smoking around 1975 for about four and a half years. Then as a result of stress and incidents at work I started again. It was just so easy, we were sitting around in meeting and somebody passed a packet of cigarettes around, and I just forgot the previous four and a half years and took one. And the next day bought a packet and carried on again. So I know how easy it is to go back.

This comes back to tension and triggers (see page 79). Stress at work raised John's tension, which meant that only a small trigger was needed to tip him into action – in this case smoking a cigarette. This is very common when people come to stop smoking – the pressure to stop has been building up inside and it only takes the tiniest nudge to turn this into action.

When I stopped finally it was prompted by the fact that my wife and I both had the flu. We were non compos mentis for about ten days. We were delirious with proper flu (not the cold people often call the flu). We came out of that and said: 'Well, we haven't smoked for over a fortnight, let's just not start again.' And that's what we did, and we've not

The previous quit had been successful so there was no need to do anything different.

looked back. That was ten years ago. I don't think I did anything particularly different the time I eventually managed to stop properly. Afterwards we probably ate more, and each put on some weight. I've lost most of that now. We got bits of advice from GPs about cutting down on eating. We probably drank a bit more as well.

We didn't seek any professional support – we supported each other. If I had a craving, I just resisted. We both did. We talked it through and we just stopped smoking. It was mutual support, which is easier when you live with someone – it's harder when you're on your own.

If you have a supportive relationship and do it together, it can obviously help.

I could never see myself going back to smoking. I'm too entrenched in my opposition to smoking now to go back! But I feel like a smoker who's not practising. In the way they talk about alcoholics. I'm pretty sure it's the same kind of addiction. An alcoholic is always an alcoholic, it's just that they're not practising after they've given up drinking.

John has a very strong 'ex-smoker' identity (Ingredient 2), which should keep him safe from relapse.

The best bit of advice I would give to a smoker trying to stop is: just do it. Stop. And use whatever props you need – seek some help and assistance.

I agree. It is unlikely to be just one thing that stops you going back – it will be all the ingredients of your formula.

A third explanation is that our group programme was already providing enough social support for the smokers so that they didn't need any more.

I think the last of these explanations is most likely. That's because I think there is a reasonable evidence that group members are already having a profound effect on each other in a way that may mask any attempt to boost motivation by buddying people up. An example of this is a phenomenon we typically find in group programmes. We call it the 'group effect'. What we find is that groups tend to do either very well or very badly. In other words, there is some kind of group dynamic going on which means, if things are going well, it affects all the members of the group in a positive way, and if things get off to a shaky start, all the members suffer from it and they tend to cave in.

So what can I tell you? If you have someone you want to stop with – your partner for example – and you are both very committed to stopping, then by all means go for it. I suspect it will only work if it feels natural for you to do this rather than forcing it on your partner or friend.

Collective quitting

Even if you don't deliberately get together with a partner or buddy, quitting can be contagious. A study in the US looked at social networks of smokers and found that smokers tended to quit in clusters. What this says to me is that the more visible everyone's quitting is, the more likely it is that it will spread, and the more it spreads, the easier it will be. You may find that if you try to quit, someone else in your group will get the idea to do the same and, if that happens, you have the beginnings of a movement!

October 2012 saw the first of a national experiment on collective quitting called 'Stoptober'. The idea was to get as many people in England to start quitting on 1 October and aim to stay smoke-free for the whole month – as a launch pad for quitting forever.

My research team evaluated the effect of this and I have to admit I was surprised how large it was. It really captured people's imagination and loads more people quit in that month than had done in previous years. If you are reading this just before October, you might want to join in with this movement.

Of course not everyone likes to join in with things, and if quitting on your own is your thing, that is absolutely fine. As always: I guide – you decide.

Chapter 13

Avoiding Temptation

Now I want to turn your attention to ways of avoiding battles that you don't need to fight. I'm going to tell you how you can reduce your risk of going back to smoking by avoiding – for a while at least – the things that are likely to trigger those cravings for a cigarette. These ingredients are particularly important at the beginning of your quit attempt and will help you get a good start.

A lot of the ingredients in this part of the book have only one star, which means that we don't have as much evidence for them as I would like. It's a reminder to me that there is still a lot of research to be done.

Ingredient 19: Change your daily routine

Rating: ★ ★

There is no direct evidence on this, but we have found that those stop-smoking advisors who help their smokers to change their routines tend to get better success rates.

In Chapter 1, I explained that one of the things nicotine does is to attach the urges to smoke to situations in which you would normally smoke. It does this by plugging in to your brain's reward circuitry: it makes your animal brain pay attention to what you were doing just before the nicotine hit, and trains it to believe that it will be rewarded if it does the same thing again the next time you come across the same situation.

It's completely unconscious and automatic. The urges usually don't come about because you start thinking, 'Wouldn't it be wonderful to have a cigarette right now?' It's just an urge that has been created by association with the situation.

Obviously what that suggests is that you're going to experience stronger urges to smoke in situations where you would normally light up. Nowadays, with smoking bans, this tends to mean particular times. For instance, when you go out for a drink, stand at a bus stop, in the car or after a meal.

So what will help you avoid those cravings? Avoiding the situations which trigger them. Have a look at the situations where you normally smoke, and see which of them you can avoid. You won't be able to cut them out altogether because they are part of your life and part of your routine, but if you can make a plan to dodge as many of them as possible in the first week or so, and certainly in the first few days, then you'll give yourself a better fighting chance.

Some people think that maybe it's best to expose yourself to these situations so that the cravings can extinguish, but the evidence is that this isn't the best way to do it. You'll have plenty of time later on to put yourself in those situations when your brain has recovered a bit from the effects of the nicotine. So, for the time being, think about situations where you would normally smoke, and see which ones you can avoid.

How do we know that changing the daily routines help? Well, it's partly from the theory I explain above, but there's also more practical evidence. When we look at which stop-smoking services are more effective than others, we find that the ones in which the advisors are instructed to recommend that smokers change their daily routine are more successful. So there is some evidence this can help.

To help you decide what routines you might be able to change, go back to the situations in which you said you smoked in the questionnaire on page 39. Now go through each one and see if you can think of a way of changing your routine so that you avoid that situation, or if you can't avoid it entirely, do things a bit differently.

For example, if you normally smoke while standing at a bus stop waiting for a bus, try a different stop, or try getting to work by train. If there is no way of avoiding that particular stop, then stand in a different place. This may seem a bit silly, but remember, while you might be clever, your animal brain is quite stupid. It will just notice that the images coming from your eyes are not the same as usual, so it will be less of a trigger for the smoking urges.

If you normally have a cigarette sitting at the table after your evening meal, get up and clear the things away and get on with something else. If you smoke in the car while listening to the radio, change the channel.

If we were sitting together I could go through each of your routines and discuss with you whether it's possible to change them and how you could do this. Unfortunately we're not, so it will be up to you to come up with other ideas. However you could always try talking to friends and family about it. And if you are seeing a stop-smoking advisor it should be one of the things they focus on at your first visit.

Ingredient 20: Avoid smokers for a while

Rating: ★

Smokers can be a big trigger to smoking – even if they do not offer you cigarettes. I don't have good evidence that avoiding smokers will help, and I realise that it might not be easy, but I think it is worth thinking about.

Imagine if you didn't know any smokers at all – how much easier it would be to stop? So many smokers slip up because someone else is lighting up or going outside for a cigarette and it is the easiest thing in the world to join them.

A lot of successful ex-smokers say they tried to keep the risk of this happening down to a minimum by avoiding people they knew who were smokers. I can't tell you about any studies that have looked at this, but it makes sense to try it if you can.

Sarah – 29 years old – *battled through the cravings*

Sarah is married with two little boys. One is two and a half and the other is eight months. She works as a support worker for young people who've come out of foster care.

I smoked my first cigarette when I was about 12. I probably started smoking every day from about 14 onwards.

Sarah is an early starter, which is typically linked to higher levels of addiction.

I started smoking at school. It was peer pressure, wanting to be cool. The first cigarette I had was made out of my dad's pipe tobacco and an envelope end. I don't understand how that didn't stop me ever smoking again. I think I must have been destined to be a smoker.

Even if the first experience seems unpleasant, nicotine is working on your animal brain to get you to do it again.

I smoked for ten years and I didn't think about stopping until I was pregnant. It was my first pregnancy that led me to give up – about three months in.

Sarah sounds like she was a contented smoker until the stimulus of pregnancy came into play.

I would try to not have a cigarette when I woke up in the morning. And I would just try to push back the time I had a cigarette. Because I found that if I had a cigarette first thing in the morning I'd want another one and another one. But it was easier to push it back as much as possible until I was just having one or two cigarettes in the evening.

Stopping gradually in this way is usually less successful than doing it abruptly, but everyone is different and this method clearly worked for Sarah.

After I'd pushed it back as far as possible I said, 'Right, I'm going to stop now completely,' so I was only really reliant on having two cigarettes a day.

Making a clear commitment is very important.

And the next day I stopped and it was really, really tough, and the day after that was even tougher, but I knew that if I did smoke I'd have to go through the day before. And then the third day was really, really, really tough, but I knew that if I started smoking again I'd just have to go through the last two days again.

You'd think that only smoking two cigarettes a day would have made it easier, but Sarah will have smoked those cigarettes much harder, so it would be more like smoking ten per day.

And then on the fourth day I stopped really needing a fag all the time and it always being on my mind, and being really upset about the fact that I couldn't smoke. So it was only really three days of hard-core cravings. On the fourth day I would just get pangs of it three or four times a day – like after I ate.

Sarah is using Ingredient 3 – taking it one day at a time – to hang in there with the incessant cravings.

And then after probably three weeks I noticed that I hadn't thought about having a cigarette for a while. Occasionally I'd think, 'Oh I'd love to have a cigarette,' but then it would go away really quickly.

The sea of craving has turned into puddles. But remember that a person can drown in just seven inches of water!

And then it was probably six months until I stopped thinking about it at all. But prior to that I'd only think about it once a week, or something like that.

My research shows that it is common still to be having smoking urges after six months.

I had to quit coffee for a while, because if I drank coffee I instantly wanted to smoke something.

Sarah is using Ingredient 19 here in avoiding a smoking situation that creates the impulse to smoke.

When I was pregnant I couldn't go out drinking, but after my pregnancy I realised that if I went out for a drink it made me want to smoke. So I think if people are just quitting for quitting, rather than quitting because they're pregnant, they should avoid alcohol for a bit.

Alcohol has brought an end to so many quit attempts. Sarah has rightly spotted this risk and taken steps to avoid it (Ingredient 21).

I'm trying to convince my husband to quit. I don't really work in an office situation where everyone goes out for a fag and I'm left out.

Having a partner who smokes is always going to make it more difficult to stay off cigarettes. Quitting with a friend or family member can provide extra support (Ingredient 18).

I will never go back to smoking. I think being a non-smoker is great. It's cheaper and I don't smell like fags, and I'll probably live a bit longer, or at least a bit more comfortably.

Sarah has taken on the identity of an ex-smoker and I expect this to help protect her against relapse (Ingredient 2).

Looking back on my time as a smoker, smoking was a part of my life at that point. But I think when you've got children you need to start thinking long-term about your health and your future. If you smoke past your twenties, you end up very old and haggard looking. I'd urge everyone to stop before they're 30.

How you do this is another matter. Have a think about the smokers you know and whether you are going to be meeting up with any of them in the next week. Can you put it off or meet somewhere you know you won't be able to smoke? If you can't avoid them, or really don't want to, have your script ready for what you will say (see Ingredient 16).

research

How easy is it to avoid other smokers?

I carried out a survey of a representative sample of smokers in England and found that 23 per cent of them lived with another smoker, 43 per cent had a few close friends who smoked, 25 per cent had a lot of friends who smoked, 15 per cent had a few workmates who smoked and 5 per cent had a lot of workmates who smoked.

What this tells me is that for quite a lot of you it may not be very difficult to avoid other smokers for a while.

The smoking ban

I don't know what you think, but most smokers and just about every non-smoker I know are delighted that we have a ban on smoking in indoor public areas. I love rock music, blues and jazz, and in my younger days, even as a non-smoker, I couldn't imagine going into a club and breathing fresh air. It would just be too weird. Then I went to a smokefree jazz club to listen to a band that played 'swing' music from the 1930s (I'm a big fan of Django Reinhardt and Stéphane Grappelli) in the Les Halles quarter in Paris, of all places – long before anyone was even considering legislation about this – and it was wonderful …

Now of course it would be horrible to have to put up with smoke in a bar, restaurant or club. Many thousands of non-smokers' lives have already been saved by the indoor smoking ban. That is because breathing other people's smoke used to trigger a lot of heart attacks.

The tobacco industry claimed that smokers would smoke more at home after the ban came in. As you can probably testify, nothing could be further from the truth. Smokers in their droves have started making their homes smokefree. And children are far less exposed to smoke from parents than they used to be.

On the other end of the scale, a lot of people thought that the indoor smoking ban would mean the end of smoking – that smokers would stop in their thousands because smoking would become too inconvenient. Actually what happened was something quite different. Sure enough, at the time the ban came into force in July 2007 a few more smokers tried to stop. But then the numbers trying to stop actually decreased below what they were the previous year. It was as though there was some kind of reaction to the ban. In fact, in the surveys done by my team, we found that smokers who reported that it was 'getting more difficult to smoke these days' were *less* likely to try to stop.

This is a well-known psychological phenomenon called 'reactance'. It's a complex word for something I'm sure you know all about: someone puts pressure on you to do something and you go completely the other way.

But that is only part of the story. In fact there was a steep decline in smoking after the ban. That's right – even though the numbers of people trying to stop actually went down, smoking rates fell. How could this be? What seemed to be happening is that the smoking ban was *helping those who were trying to stop succeed.* So smokers who wanted to quit, for whatever reason, found it easier immediately after the ban than beforehand.

This fits with everything I've been saying about smoking triggers. Imagine you are sitting in a bar trying not to smoke and there are people smoking around you. You are constantly being exposed to these triggers, and it is the easiest thing in the world just to give in to the desire, reach over and light up. After the smoking ban, those triggers were moved outside. In fact, ironically, the very places that would have triggered smoking in the past are now associated with not smoking. Bars, restaurants and clubs of today have become like the supermarkets and churches of yesterday.

Okay, what does this tell us about what you can do to keep from smoking? The lesson I draw is that, even if it isn't feasible for you to completely avoid friends who smoke for a while, you can make the smokefree laws work in your favour as long as you start out with a clear plan – for example you definitely won't go outside when your friends go for a smoke.

Ingredient 21: Avoid alcohol for a while

Rating: ★

We do not have direct evidence that cutting down on alcohol helps with stopping smoking, but so many smokers report relapsing after a few drinks, and we know that alcohol lowers your inhibitions, so it makes sense to minimise your alcohol consumption at least for a week or two after you first quit.

Two thirds of adults in Britain drink alcohol at least weekly, and the figure for smokers is higher. A quarter of adults drink more than is safe (three units per day for men and two for women – a unit being a half-pint glass of 3-4% strength beer or two-thirds of a small glass of wine). In fact one in five smokers in Britain is alcohol-dependent using the standard definition. (I know – that does seem surprisingly high but smokers are more likely to drink a lot of alcohol than non-smokers!)

This book is not about drinking – that is a whole other thing – but drinking and smoking are so closely connected that if you drink, it is worth looking at how you can change your drinking patterns so that it boosts your chances of stopping smoking.

There are two reasons why drinking alcohol can make it more difficult to stop smoking: one is that it undermines self-control and the other is that it provides a smoking trigger. For both these reasons, drinking alcohol may not be the best idea for a week or two. I can't tell you for sure that it will make a difference to your chances of staying off cigarettes, but it might.

Perhaps this is something that you can decide from your own experience. You know how much you drink (if you drink at all) and what effect it has on you. You probably also know from when you have tried to stop smoking before how much it affects your self-control. I'm not telling you to go teetotal forever, but cutting down for a few weeks can be sensible.

Ingredient 22: Go to bed early

Rating: ★

If you are asleep, you can't smoke – that much is certain! I find that, early on, a lot of smokers go to bed early to escape the need to smoke. I can't tell you for sure that this will work for you, but it could.

Early in the quit attempt, evenings can be very difficult indeed. You may well be thinking about cigarettes all the time – like a gnawing hunger in the pit of your stomach. If you are using nicotine products you should have no hesitation in using as much as you like to dampen down that feeling. But, even so, it can be quite tough.

In that situation a lot of people just go to bed early. It can be a blessed relief. If you don't normally smoke in bed, then the simple fact that you are in a situation where you never smoke can also help – even if you just read or listen to the radio rather than going to sleep.

It may feel a bit odd going to bed at 9 p.m. but, remember, you are on a mission and only one thing matters – avoiding that fateful puff.

Ingredient 23: Get rid of all remaining cigarettes

Rating: ★

Stop-smoking advisors will generally tell you to throw away your cigarettes and get rid of your ashtrays. We don't know for sure that this helps, but it does make good sense.

I sometimes come across people who are stopping smoking who say that they like to keep a cigarette in their pocket or handbag because it makes it easier not to smoke if they know there is one nearby if they want it.

I am not aware of any studies on this, but I slightly worry about this tactic. One thing we know about human nature is that the easier something is to do, the more likely we are to do it. The stop-smoking advisors I know will mostly tell you to get rid of all your cigarettes to keep temptation as far away from you as possible. And that is my advice to you. But I realise that you may be different.

And perhaps it doesn't matter. Perhaps when you decide you are going to have a cigarette, nothing short of an earthquake is going to stop you. One of my researchers, Dr Eleni Vangeli, found something like that. She asked people who had lasted at least a month but then gone back to smoking about what happened. She found that most of them didn't decide to go back to smoking at all – they thought they would just have one or two cigarettes, perhaps a pack, and then would carry on not smoking, but it didn't work out like that.

This probably sounds familiar to you. What surprised Eleni and me was that the lapse was often quite pre-meditated: they actually went out and bought a packet of cigarettes so that they could smoke. They had made a clear decision and gone from 'I will not have a single puff' to 'I'll just have one cigarette now'. It made no difference that they didn't have a cigarette to hand. So, once again, we see the crucial importance of that personal rule. *Not one puff.*

Chapter 14

Dealing with Cravings

So far you've found a suit of armour to protect you. You've decided whether you are going to use some form of expert support in the form of professional advice, self-help materials, nicotine products and medicines. In your battle to become smoke-free, you have weakened your enemy. You've decided on your tactics for staying strong and ways of avoiding battles you don't have to fight.

Now we get to the part where you choose your weapons for those battles you can't avoid: when you are going to have to fight back against the cravings.

This chapter tells you about ways that you can deal with the temptations or urges to smoke when they occur. There are lots of things you can do, but research from my friend and colleague Professor Saul Shiffman in the United States strongly suggests that the most important thing is to do *something*. Don't just wait and hope that it goes away.

The other thing Professor Shiffman found was that while sometimes cravings come on suddenly, sometimes you get quite a lot of warning. There is a period where you kind of know that things are getting worse. When that happens it is important not to ignore it – you have to act to stop what could turn into a downward spiral.

Ingredient 24: Get active

Rating: ★ ★

There is strong evidence that walking or just doing some form of physical activity that gets your heart rate up a bit reduces desire for a cigarette. The effect is similar to what you get from using one of the nicotine products. So if you experience a strong urge to smoke and you can go out for a short walk, I would recommend it.

When I was at school, smoking was closely tied to team sports. I played rugby and most of the time would light up after a match. That was a long time ago. But since the 1990s there has been research showing that children doing individual sports, such as athletics, are less likely to smoke than average, but those doing team sports are more likely to be smokers.

In general, though, smokers are less likely to do sports or physical activities for health or fun than non-smokers. If you are an exception to the rule, that is good news! Professor Michael Ussher at St George's University of London and I did one of the first studies to show that physical activity is very good at controlling cravings. In fact just light physical activity such as walking and pedalling on an exercise bicycle seems to have more effect on cigarette cravings than chewing a piece of nicotine gum.

The effect of physical activity on cravings is quite short-lived though. And studies that have tried to see whether physical activity helps you quit long-term have struggled to show any benefit.

So here's the conundrum: even light physical activity definitely reduces your desire to smoke – certainly while you are doing it and for a short time afterwards. But when we test whether putting you through your paces in an exercise programme helps you stop long-term we can't seem to find an effect.

Here's what I think is going on. Exercise does reduce cravings, and this is fine if you can go for a walk or do something active when the cravings strike, but very often you can't. What is more, forcing yourself to get physically active is in itself quite a challenge and takes a certain amount of self-control. That might use up some of the mental reserves needed to keep you off cigarettes.

If this is correct, then I suspect that getting active is only going to be something that will work for you if you already have a routine going – i.e. you already go for walks, go to the gym, go running or play sport – or if you are attracted to the idea of making this a new part of your life and identity (see Ingredient 2 for more on this).

If either of these applies to you, then give serious thought to developing a physical activity routine for when the cravings strike. You won't be able to use it all the time and so will definitely need other ingredients. But it could help. However, if you can't face the thought of taking up an exercise regime at the same time as quitting, another tactic might work better for you.

The final thing to say about becoming physically active of course is that it will be good for your mental and physical health anyway, so there's nothing to be lost by trying it. And it could help to keep the weight off if you find your appetite increases.

Ingredient 25: Isometric exercises

Rating: ★ ★

Even just sitting in a chair and tensing and relaxing the muscles in your legs and arms can reduce the cravings for a cigarette.

When I was a schoolboy I remember seeing advertisements in comics and magazines for how to become a 'he-man'. There would be a picture of some skinny kid at the beach and the bullies would kick sand in his face, but then he would 'work out' using an amazing isometric muscle-building machine and the next thing you know he would be kicking sand in the bullies' faces! I remember thinking that the beach seemed a pretty dangerous place.

'Isometric' exercises are ones where you don't actually move your body. Instead you tense your muscles and make them work against each other, keeping the bits of your body exactly where they are. The advantage of this is that you can do these exercises any time, anywhere and in any position.

Thinking about the difficulties of going for a walk or getting on an exercise bike whenever the cravings strike, I wondered whether you could get the same effect using isometric exercises. And it turns out you can.

Your one-minute isometric exercise workout

You can do this exercise sitting in a chair – whether at home, at work, in a restaurant or anywhere else.

1 Pay attention to your breathing and don't forget to keep doing it – in other words, don't hold your breath but keep breathing steadily in and out.
2 Now tense up the muscles in your calves (the lower part of your legs) for ten seconds, then let go for five seconds. Feel the tension, but try not to let any physical movement show. See if you can do it without anyone noticing anything. (Count the ten seconds in your head as 'one little second, two little seconds, three little seconds, etc.' There is no need to look at your watch.)
3 Now do it again.
4 Now move on to your thighs. Tense the top and bottom of your thighs so that they stay completely still, but the muscles are working against each other. Count ten seconds and concentrate on keeping the muscles tense while trying to look relaxed in your face so that no one notices. And remember to keep breathing. After ten seconds relax for five seconds.
5 Then repeat this.

If you want to vary it, you can tense your buttocks or your stomach muscles. You could try your arms too, but they will shake so you might not want to do that in public.

Remember this is not the only thing you can do to tackle cravings. But if you find that it works for you, do it as often as you need to.

Exercise and stopping smoking

My colleague Professor Michael Ussher and I looked at what happens if you just go for a walk to help with the craving. Does it help? The answer is yes.

But you can't always go for a walk. You might be sitting in a meeting or at home minding the baby, and it just wouldn't be practical to get up and start hiking. So we were interested to find out if you could get the same effect by using 'isometric exercises'. Body builders used to use these (some still do) to build up muscle strength without having to move the muscles at all. (The fitness coach Dave Hubbard has a good 90-second workout you can easily find online.)

We created a set of muscle tension and relaxation exercises and did an experiment to see if it would help with the cravings. We recruited around 60 smokers, half of whom would be randomly chosen to try the isometric exercises, and the other half would be in the control condition.

Those who would be doing the isometric exercises were instructed to do ten minutes of muscle control and relaxation; whereas those in the control condition were instructed to simply focus their attention on the muscles, but not do anything with them. This is because we wanted to give these smokers something to concentrate on to make sure that the isometric exercises didn't stop the cravings simply because they distracted their attention.

We found that those who did the muscle tension and relaxation did have quite a bit less craving – for the duration of the exercise and for a little while afterwards – than those in the control condition. So I think we can be pretty confident this kind of activity can help with the craving. It's certainly something that I'd recommend – it's very easy to do, it doesn't cost anything and could help.

Ingredient 26: Glucose tablets

Rating: ★ ★

Glucose tablets, or possibly a glucose drink, have been shown in experiments to reduce the desire to smoke. There is one RCT showing an effect on short-term abstinence, and one large RCT showed that it might boost success rates in people using nicotine products or Zyban (buproprion).

The jury is still out on the benefits for lasting success but – given how cheap these tablets are and that we know they do reduce desire to smoke – I have given them two stars.

Glucose is a form of sugar. Your body turns all carbohydrates into glucose so that it can use it for energy. Sugar that you put in your tea or coffee or on cereal, otherwise known as sucrose, is made up of a mixture of glucose and fructose.

Back in the 1980s I was interviewing smokers for a study and some of them talked about the feeling they got when they couldn't smoke for a day. They described it as like 'hunger' – like a physical feeling in the pit of their stomach.

As a psychologist, I was aware that it is easy for us to mislabel feelings based on what we expect to feel. For example, there is research showing that people can be made to think they are physically attracted to someone if we prompt them to feel a bit anxious when meeting them. They can interpret the anxiety as attraction. Panic attacks are another example: sufferers experience profound physiological effects that they interpret as a sense of doom, which starts a vicious cycle until a full-blown panic attack occurs. In reality the symptoms are caused by physiological changes that may have nothing to do with anxiety or panic, and it can help prevent the cycle to do things that control the physiological effects (such as breath control).

What the smokers were telling me gave me an idea though – perhaps the craving symptoms the smokers were experiencing were in fact 'hunger'. And perhaps that hunger was caused by low blood sugar. I now think I was wrong about the blood sugar – we looked at blood sugar levels of smokers after they had quit and they were fine. But the link between hunger and cigarette craving was too important to let go, so we set up some studies to test the idea.

In the first study, smokers attending the Maudsley Hospital smokers' clinic who had already been off cigarettes for a week were given either glucose tablets or a low-calorie sweet to chew for the next week. When they came back we asked them to rate their urges to smoke using the same scale that you filled in on page 44. We got the questionnaires back and, I'll be honest – I didn't look at them for ages. I'd gone off the idea and thought it seemed a bit crazy. How could chewing glucose tablets reduce craving for a cigarette? What had I been thinking?

Anyway, a few weeks later I had a pile of student essays to mark – not my preferred way of spending an evening – so I started looking for something else to do. I came across the pile of questionnaires from the glucose study and began to leaf through them – and my jaw dropped! Even without doing statistical analysis it was clear that something interesting was going on. The people who were chewing glucose tablets seemed to have much lower craving levels than those using the low-calorie sweets.

I got together with my team and we did the full analysis and published the findings. That set off a series of studies in which we showed that there was a near-immediate effect of chewing glucose tablets compared with a low-calorie sweet. (You had to chew a few of them at a time though.) We also showed that chewing glucose tablets could help smokers to stay off cigarettes for at least four weeks.

So we set up a very large study to see whether glucose tablets could help smokers stop for longer than that – for at least six months. It was quite a tall order for a number of reasons. The biggest problem of course is that we couldn't stop our smokers from eating sugar contained in other foods, so those not given the glucose tablets might just eat more of those foods to compensate. Half of the smokers in our study also used either nicotine products or Zyban so we were able to see whether the glucose tablets could have an effect on top of those methods of support.

The results were disappointing. Overall the difference in six-month success rates between the glucose tablets and the calorie-free sweets was too small for us to be confident there was any meaningful effect. On the other hand, the glucose tablets did seem to help those people who were already taking a nicotine product or Zyban. So perhaps there was something there after all.

No one else has tried to repeat this study, so where we stand right now is that we know glucose tablets can help with cravings and we think it might help with long-term success at stopping, but we can't be confident.

So what can I advise you? The tablets are very cheap and they might help, so if you feel like trying them there is little to be lost.

Weight and health concerns

Some of my colleagues were worried that giving people glucose tablets to chew might make them put on even more weight than they would have put on anyway. But I noticed that in fact the number of calories in these tablets was very low – a whole packet of tablets had no more calories than a slice of bread. The reason the tablets take the edge off the hunger is that the glucose gets directly into the bloodstream making your brain think it has had a big meal.

This led me to think that glucose tablets might actually help you lose weight rather than gain it. So I did a small study to see whether this might be true. I advertised for people who wanted to lose weight to take part in an experiment in which they either chewed glucose tablets or calorie-free sweets for two weeks. My idea was that those chewing the glucose tablets would naturally lose weight because they would feel full more and so eat less of other foods. As I predicted, the volunteers chewing the glucose tablets lost weight while those chewing the calorie-free sweets did not. All this happened completely naturally, without them thinking about it – I told them not to make any special effort to limit what they ate.

So, far from glucose causing more weight gain in people trying to stop smoking, it looks as though it might lead to less weight gain.

Now you might imagine that perhaps I had discovered a great way of losing weight: eat sugar! Weight control is not my area of study and my results are too preliminary to make any such claim. But I can say that you shouldn't worry that by chewing glucose tablets you'll pile on the pounds.

The other worry that some people have about chewing glucose tablets is the effect it might have on the teeth. I have been advised by dentists, however, that chewing glucose tablets for a few weeks won't have any lasting effects, especially if you remember to brush your teeth properly with fluoride toothpaste.

Ingredient 27: Mental exercises

Rating: ★ ★

The way you think affects the way you feel. There are some well-known 'thinking' therapies that can help to deal with emotional problems, and some of these have been tried out as ways of helping people stop smoking.

> If you practise these yourself, they might help you fight off the temptations to smoke, or at least put you mentally in a better position to do that. The most well known of these therapies are 'CBT' (which stands for cognitive behavioural therapy) and 'mindfulness' training. Another mental technique, which I will call 're-imagining', has been found to be helpful in people suffering from post-traumatic stress disorder and could potentially be effective in resisting cravings.

Sometimes it seems that we think too much. I remember a teacher at my boarding school telling me that the masters tried to keep us doing as much as possible because the last thing they wanted was for us to sit around thinking. We might get it into our heads to start a revolution!

But thinking is what gives us the edge over other animals. It has meant that we can build civilisations, and it is what allows you to decide that you don't want to smoke any more, and then stick to that decision.

Some special ways of retraining the way we think about things may help you with this. I have included three of them in this ingredient. I don't expect you to use them all at the same time – that might be a bit much. If I were you, I'd choose one that appeals the most and give that a good go. If, at some time in the future, you find yourself smoking again, you could try one of the others. Of course, if you like them all and think you can manage it – I wouldn't want to stop you.

One thing I would say: all three of these mental exercises have been found to be helpful in dealing with distress and mood disorders, so – as with everything in this book – there really is no downside to trying them.

CBT

CBT has become a bit of a catch-all term used for any problem-solving approach to psychological or behavioural problems. However, when I talk about CBT in this section, I am referring to a limited set of specific mental techniques.

I would not be doing you or CBT experts any favours in pretending that I could tell you how to do DIY CBT in a few short paragraphs. So instead I will tell you about some of the components of CBT that you *might* be able to use. I won't use the technical names but instead will focus on what they are and how they may help.

> 'CBT' is the abbreviation given to a very popular form of mood and behaviour control called cognitive behavioural therapy. It involves retraining you to think differently about things so that you feel and act differently. There are many books and websites that explain how you can do this. If you suffer from a mood disorder, it is better to go to a trained clinical psychologist but, as you may have found out, it is not always easy to get to see one.

Re-thinking your cravings

When you experience an urge to smoke it comes with a lot of baggage. The same physical experience can be positive or negative, depending on how you interpret it. You might be able to re-think the experience so that it becomes a positive sign that your body is re-adjusting to life without cigarettes. The technique is all about reframing your approach to problems so as to think about them in a more useful way. For example: what does it mean to be feeling a craving? You could think of it as weakness. But what about seeing it as a positive: as a sign that you are succeeding in not smoking and are making progress, and that every bout of cravings you fight off is another battle won and a step closer to the day when you stop feeling them at all?

Re-thinking and combating stress

I said in Chapter 1 that smoking does not help with stress but only appears to. This is because, as a smoker, you go through repeated cycles of stress caused by nicotine withdrawal followed by relief when you smoke. So naturally your animal brain associates smoking with stress relief and your human brain comes to believe that smoking helps with stress. This means that you could benefit from re-training yourself so that instead of reaching for a cigarette whenever you are stressed, you do something that will actually help.

Progressive muscle relaxation exercise

A simple relaxation method that I like goes like this. You can do it for between 5 and 20 minutes and in any position – lying down, sitting up or even standing:

1 Pay attention to the muscles of your face and neck. Start with your forehead; when you breathe out, let the muscle go, relaxing it completely. Then work your way down and around all of the muscles in your face and neck, relaxing each muscle more and more on each exhale. Don't forget the muscles around your eyes and your eyelids.

2 Focus all your attention on this. Let it fill your mind, leaving no space for other thoughts. Don't battle with those other thoughts and feelings. Just let them pass. Focus on relaxing your muscles with each out-breath.

3 Enjoy the feeling of relaxation and being in the moment. Forget the past, and the future. There will be plenty of time when you have finished to sort out problems of the future. The only thing that matters at the moment is just relaxing your muscles with every out-breath.

4 Allow any tension and worries to fade into the background; don't force them away – just let them disappear because you've got something more important to do just for the moment, which is to relax.

5 Every time a new unpleasant thought pops into your mind, don't worry – that's natural – just go back to thinking about relaxing your muscles and let the thought fade out again.

6 Now move to your shoulders, arms and back. Do the same thing as before. Moving around your body, seek out tension and relax it with every out-breath. Focus all your attention in the moment on what you are doing and allow other thoughts and feelings to fade away each time they pop into your mind.

7 Some part of you will be monitoring the time and thinking, 'It's time to stop now,' or, 'I wonder how long I've been going.' This can be a bit distracting, so you might want to set a timer or a piece of music of the right duration so that you can relax completely without having to worry about it.

This is just one approach, and you may well come across others that would work for you. The key elements common to all approaches are:

- Paying attention to your muscles and gently but purposefully relaxing them, using your breathing as a kind of metronome.
- Not battling with intrusive thoughts and feelings but letting them fade each time they occur by focusing on relaxation and breathing.
- Staying in the moment and putting thoughts about the past and the future out of your mind just while you are doing this – this is your time when nothing else matters.

Relaxation exercises are a tried-and-tested method of stress control. There are many different methods, and you can look them up on the Internet, get a book from the local library or get a booklet from your health centre.

Countering defeatism

In stories of people dying of hypothermia, you hear about how the end comes when they give up and allow themselves to drift off – it is easier than fighting to stay alive. The same is true with stopping smoking. It is easy to accept defeat – to start thinking negative thoughts and to lose the will to continue. If you know that this is starting to happen, you can retrain the way you think by countering these self-defeating thoughts every time with strong positive statements to yourself that you are doing well, that you have the strength and you will succeed.

Self-reward

CBT recognises the importance of reward and punishment in controlling our behaviour. Praise and blame are important rewards and punishers. Sometimes we blame ourselves and punish our own mistakes, when we would do better to reward our successes.

I'm guilty of this when I play squash. If I play a bad shot I get angry with myself and tell myself off! Then I think how stupid that is and tell myself off for that. Next thing I know, I've lost the match – and I tell myself off for that … It's a good thing my animal brain has such a short memory because when next the time comes to play, I'm all optimistic again about the prospect of winning – the proverbial triumph of hope over experience.

CBT proposes a different approach. Instead of telling yourself off and thinking of yourself as hopeless and useless when things go wrong, you reward yourself all those many times when things go right. You can plan treats for yourself at the end of every day that you don't smoke. Every time you come through a bout of craving without giving in, say well done to yourself and allow yourself to feel proud of each small victory.

Mindfulness

> 'Mindfulness' involves paying attention to your feelings but detaching yourself from them so that they become empty and without meaning. There is a little bit of evidence that doing this with the need for a cigarette can reduce the cravings.

You know the odd sensation you get when you say a word over and over again until it ceases to have any meaning? I had it the other day when I was being filmed talking about smoking, and the producer had me saying the lines again and again and again … It got to the point where I could have been talking Japanese. The words meant nothing to me.

What's going on? The explanation that rings true for me is that the little brain cells that represent the meaning of the words get tired – just like a muscle gets tired when you keep using it – and they give up. So you can say the words, but your brain is not able to experience the full richness of their meaning because the brain cells are overworked and need a rest.

Of course, they soon recover. But it tells us something interesting. It is possible to detach the part of your mind that interprets sensations and physical experiences so that they don't mean anything.

An old school friend told me that he had experienced something similar when 'tripping' on LSD. He had gone out into the woods with friends on a very cold winter's day with snow on the ground and ponds frozen over. It was not a day that one would want to venture out without a thick coat and gloves, but he was only wearing his school uniform. What he told me was that he 'knew' it was bitterly cold. He had the sensations of cold. But it didn't carry any meaning for him so it wasn't unpleasant – it was just something that he noticed.

Mindfulness aims to get a similar effect – although without using illegal drugs – simply by controlling your thought processes. With mindfulness, you don't fight against the urges to smoke, the anxiety, the depression and so forth. You *accept* them and observe them. You focus on them and allow the brain cells that experience the meaning of them to tire out so that they don't matter.

That's the crux of it. You experience cravings, but they don't matter.

This is all very new and there's a little bit of research suggesting it might help in the case of smoking. There is more research that this kind of approach can help some people who suffer from chronic pain, anxiety or depression.

Re-imagining

One thing you can do when you fancy a cigarette or feel a strong need to smoke is to go through a routine in your mind in which you imagine yourself smoking, making it as real as possible. You imagine the feel of the cigarette in your fingers and the feeling of the smoke as it goes down your throat and into your lungs. You then imagine how you feel afterwards when you find that you have lapsed – and wasted everything you have put into the quit attempt so far ... Except that you haven't – because you didn't actually smoke. So you can use this feeling of disgust to stop you lighting up in the first place. I don't know that this will help stop you from smoking, but it might.

With stopping smoking, as with other areas of life where we set ourselves rules, we sometimes dream that we have transgressed. When I used to be a vegetarian I would sometimes dream that I ate meat. It would be a big relief to me when I realised that it had not actually happened. Smokers trying to stop often have the same experience.

My friend and colleague Professor Peter Hajek calls these 'DAMIT dreams' (technically this is an acronym for dreams of absent-minded transgression, but the sense is clear enough!). He noticed that a lot of smokers in his clinic would report these dreams and they would be quite vivid. In the dream, the smoker would be mortified at having lapsed and, on waking, would be hugely relieved. As a scientist, Peter wondered whether this would have any effect on whether they went on to relapse to smoking in real life. He found that, perhaps surprisingly, the smokers who had DAMIT dreams were *more* likely to succeed in stopping.

Of course we don't know for sure why this should be, but one explanation is that the DAMIT dreams were enough of a punishment to deter lapsing in real life – and because it was only a dream they did not experience the chemical effect of the nicotine in rekindling their urges to smoke.

Another strand of research related to this comes from trying to help people recover from PTSD (post-traumatic stress disorder). PTSD is a debilitating psychological disorder that often occurs in those who have been involved in or witnessed severe trauma. Sufferers experience vivid flashbacks in which they relive the trauma; this can blight their lives and break up families. The research has found that encouraging sufferers to continue playing the scenario past the traumatic event itself to the aftermath, where they are okay, helps them reframe the experience. They come to appreciate at a deep emotional level that they are not under threat.

The question then is whether this could work for smokers experiencing a powerful desire for a cigarette. They are anticipating the relief and satisfaction that the cigarette will give but if they play the story forward just a little they will realise how bad they will feel at having 'blown it'.

You will probably know from your own experience that the cigarette you smoke after having stopped for a while does not even taste good and many smokers put it out halfway through. But the damage has been done.

This suggests a possible ingredient in which, when you are sorely tempted to have a cigarette, instead of actually smoking one, you try to imagine smoking it as vividly as you can, including what you will feel like afterwards. If you have tried to stop before, you will know what that first lapse felt like. You probably felt deflated and let down and did not even finish the cigarette. And you still wanted another one. I don't know, because the research has not been done, but it could be enough to stop you having that fateful puff.

Ingredient 28: Breathing exercises

Rating: ★ ★

Controlled breathing is helpful in regulating your emotions. There is now some good research showing that it can reduce your urges to smoke. I can't tell you for sure that this will make a big difference to your chances of stopping, because the studies have not been done, but the fact that it can control your urge to smoke is a promising first step.

There was a very interesting study published in one of the main science journals, *Nature*, which showed that when some people had a stroke in a particular part of their brain they seemed to lose their craving for a cigarette.

This seemed a bit odd. You can imagine how brain damage might affect addiction, but this seemed to be specific to cigarette cravings. Now I happen to think the study probably didn't show what the authors claimed, but if you look at that part of the brain they were talking about it raises some interesting possibilities. This part of the brain does a number of things, one of which is to tell you to breathe. It makes you feel the urge to breathe when the carbon dioxide level in your blood gets too high. This opened the possibility that this part of the brain is related to cigarette cravings – because the brain might mistake the effect that nicotine has on this part of the brain with a need to breathe.

Armed with this information, my colleagues and I looked at the scientific literature to see if breathing exercises could help with craving for a cigarette. We found a couple of studies suggesting that this was a promising line of study but nothing conclusive. So we set about doing our own study. We got smokers who hadn't had a cigarette since the day before to do either a set of breathing exercises or just watch a video about them without doing anything.

These were very simple breathing exercises drawn from the Indian practice of yoga. One was an abdominal breathing exercise where you slowly and deeply inhale and exhale using your abdomen. The other one was what is called alternate nostril breathing, where you close off one nostril and breathe in through the other nostril, then close off the open one and then breathe out through the other nostril.

We did see a reduction in craving in the people who were doing the exercises compared with those just watching the video. The reduction didn't last very long, but it did offer some promise. It could be a way that you can very easily and discreetly do something when you are experiencing a craving and there are no other options. So, for example, if you're sitting in a meeting or are on a train and you really feel like a cigarette, this is something you can do to help reduce cravings immediately.

I don't know whether these exercises will help you stay off cigarettes in the long term, but they might – and can't do any harm.

Abdominal breathing exercise

1   Sit upright but relaxed with your shoulders hanging loose and your back straight.
2   Breathe in by pulling your diaphragm down so that you feel your tummy expand (not your chest) for about five seconds.
3   Then breathe out by pulling up your diaphragm and feel your tummy go in for five seconds.
4   Continue breathing and notice the breath going in and out of your nostrils and the feeling of your tummy going in and out but your chest staying still. Try to fill your lungs from the bottom and empty them almost completely but without straining.
5   Do this for up to five minutes, all the time concentrating on your breathing and remembering to keep the rest of your body relaxed.

Alternate nostril breathing exercise

1   Sit upright but relaxed with your back straight. Let your shoulders hang loose.
2   Place your right thumb on your right nostril to close it off and breathe in steadily for five seconds through your left nostril.
3   Once you have filled your lungs, place the forefinger of your right hand on your left nostril to close it and release the right nostril.
4   Then breathe out steadily for five seconds through your right nostril until you have almost emptied your lungs but are not straining.
5   Next breathe in steadily for five seconds through your right nostril.
6   Then place your thumb on your right nostril, release your forefinger from the left nostril and breathe out through the left nostril.
7   Repeat this process of breathing through each nostril in turn for up to five minutes. This should feel quite relaxing and calming.

Ingredient 29: Eat healthy snacks

> ### Rating: ★
> Healthy snacks are things like fresh or dried fruit, carrot sticks or cereal bars that you can carry round with you and eat instead of smoking. I don't have good evidence that they will help you stop smoking but they could. And if you choose the right snack, it might help prevent weight gain.

I won't lie to you. The chances that you will gain weight when you stop smoking are high. If you've stopped before for any length of time you will know that anyway. I could tell you to try to keep your weight down by going on a diet – but I don't think that would help.

I'm also reassured that – and you may find this surprising – the amount of weight you put on when you stop smoking will not reduce your chances of lasting success. In fact some studies have found that the more weight people gained, the more likely they were to continue to stay off cigarettes.

But there are ways you can limit the weight gain. One of them is to carry healthy snacks around with you. Fruit is a great healthy snack. Cereal bars are okay, but check the calorie count on the packet because some of them can be quite high. Remember that on average men require 2,000 to 2,500 calories per day (if you are reasonably active) and women about 1,500 to 2,000 – so if you have a snack bar that has 300 calories, that's a lot!

Carrots are actually a pretty good healthy snack, even if they don't improve your eyesight! You have probably heard the myth about carrots improving your eyesight because they contain vitamin A. You might not know that this story was invented by the British Air Ministry during the Second World War to explain the accuracy of our night-fighter pilots. They had developed secret radar systems which guided the pilots to their targets, but didn't want the Germans to find out about them. So how did they hide this fact? They told everyone the pilots had developed night vision by eating a steady diet of carrots!

Tips for weight loss

Guess what – just like with stopping smoking, there is no single formula that will work for everyone. But there are things you can put in your 'weight-loss formula' which could do the trick for you. The evidence is nothing like as good as it is for smoking, but there is some and I think it can be summed up like this:

1 To lose weight you have to consume fewer calories than you burn. There is no getting around this. The average man burns about 2,000–2,500 calories a day and the average woman burns around 1,500–2,000.
2 To achieve this, you have to find rules you can stick to regarding your exercise and your eating.
3 Diets that are successful (at least for a while) involve finding rules you can stick to because they make the process of limiting your calories a bit easier. These include: nearly fasting for two days each week but eating what you like on the other days (the 5:2 diet); cutting out carbohydrates (the Atkins diet); regular weighing and calorie counting (the WeightWatchers approach – though they translate calories into 'points'). The evidence is that all of these approaches can work for some people for a reasonable length of time, but you probably need to refresh them or try different approaches when they start to lose their power.
4 Exercise programmes that are successful likewise involve finding ways of increasing your energy expenditure in a way that is relatively easy and fits into your life and identity. If you live near a park, then walking or jogging a couple of miles a day works well. If you use lifts a lot, then routinely taking stairs instead makes a difference.

I'll tell you what I did to lose weight (about a stone and a half) about ten years ago. It may or may not work for you. I looked up what my ideal body weight was – 72 kilogrammes. I then got some electronic scales with a digital readout. I set myself a target of eating 500 calories less per day than I was burning and weighed myself every day. I accepted that my weight would go up and down just because of fluids on a day-by-day basis, but pretty soon it was easy to see the downward trend, and that was very rewarding. I always weighed myself first thing in the morning before my cup of tea – with no clothes on obviously!

It took about three months but was relatively painless, and now I keep myself below 74 kilogrammes by weighing myself regularly and reducing my calorie intake or exercising more if I am above that weight when I wake up in the morning. This may seem like a bit of a palaver but it's part of my routine and it works for me.

Obviously there is much more to be said about losing weight, but I hope this gives you something useful to go on.

Chapter 15

Your 'QuickStop' Guide: Creating your Own SmokeFree Formula

You have arrived here because you're ready for a quit attempt. That's really great!

It may be the first one you have done with *The SmokeFree Formula*, or it may be the second or third … it doesn't matter. The principle is the same. Each time you quit, you use whatever ingredients you think will give you the best chance this time using my guidance and your own experience.

So now just follow the instructions – and good luck!

Your SmokeFree Formula chart

Use the chart below to make up your own personal formula for this quit attempt.

Use as many or as few ingredients as you like. If you are not sure whether to choose an ingredient, go to the chapter in the book that describes it and read about why you might want to pick it.

I have given each ingredient a star rating to tell you about the strength of evidence to support it. But everyone is different and you may have tried an ingredient before and found it didn't work for you. Of course that doesn't mean it won't work for you this time, but you should use whatever ingredients you have confidence in.

Just to recap, here are my star ratings:

★★★ Strong evidence it can help
★★ Some evidence it can help
★ No good evidence, but it might help

You are not tied to an ingredient if you find that it is not working for you. But I strongly advise you to give it a good go before dropping it. Go back and read the section on it because you may need to change the way you use it to make it work.

Your approach

First, let's look at how you are going to approach this quit attempt. There are several options, some of them with stronger evidence behind them than others. Any one of them might help, so choose whatever you think will work best for you.

At this quit attempt I will ...

1	stop abruptly rather than cut down gradually (see page 96) ★★★	☐
2	take 'smoker' out of my identity (see page 98) ★★	☐
3	take it one day at a time (see page 101) ★	☐

Personal advice and support

Now let's look at this section because whatever you choose here will influence the rest of your ingredients. About ten per cent of smokers in countries where it is available use professional help with stopping, but many more could definitely benefit from it.

At this quit attempt I will ...

| 4 | see a stop-smoking advisor (see page 104) ★★★ | ☐ |
| 5 | use a telephone helpline (see page 122) ★★ | ☐ |

Automated support and self-help materials

There are dozens of free websites and smartphone apps available for you to use. And there may be a text-messaging service available. You can also get hold of free stop-smoking booklets or buy another stop-smoking book.

At this quit attempt I will ...

6   use a text-messaging service (see page 124) ★★★   ❑

7   use a stop-smoking website (see page 126) ★★   ❑

8   use another stop-smoking book (see page 130) ★★   ❑

9   use a stop-smoking smartphone app (see page 131) ★   ❑

Nicotine products

There are lots of nicotine products available to buy or get from your doctor. They are safe and when used properly can really help you stop smoking. You can use them for as long as you like without fear of harm and use as much as you find necessary.

At this quit attempt I will ...

10   use one or more licensed nicotine products, e.g. skin patch (see page 134) ★★★ ❑

11   use an electronic cigarette (see page 146) ★★   ❑

Stop-smoking medicines

There are several pills you can take which are safe and can really help you stop smoking if you take them as directed. You will generally need a prescription from your doctor to get these but you might be able to get them from a nurse or pharmacist.

I will ...

12   use varenicline (Champix) (see page 156) ★★★   ❑

13   use bupropion (Zyban) (see page 160) ★★★   ❑

14   use cytisine (Tabex) (see page 161) ★★★   ❑

Staying strong

There will almost certainly be moments of weakness. Here are ingredients that you can set up in advance to strengthen your resolve.

I will ...

15   plan things to keep busy (see page 167) ★★   ❑

16   tell other people about the quit attempt (see page 167) ★   ❑

17   count the money being saved (see page 170) ★   ❑

18   quit with friends or family (see page 171) ★   ❑

Avoiding temptation

Prevention is better than cure, and it makes sense to do what you can to avoid situations that will test your resolve. These ingredients might help you do that.

I will ...

19	change my daily routine (see page 178) ★★	❑
20	try to avoid smokers for a while (see page 180) ★	❑
21	avoid alcohol for a while (see page 186) ★	❑
22	go to bed early (see page 187) ★	❑
23	get rid of all remaining cigarettes (see page 187) ★	❑

Dealing with cravings

There will be many times when you are sorely tempted to smoke. You have to do whatever it takes to avoid giving in. There are a lot of things you can try, some with quite good evidence behind them.

I will ...

24	get active (see page 190) ★★	❑
25	do 'isometric' exercises (tensing muscles) (see page 191) ★★	❑
26	chew glucose tablets (see page 193) ★★	❑
27	do mental exercises (see page 196) ★★	❑
28	do breathing exercises to control the smoking urges (see page 203) ★★	❑
29	eat healthy snacks (see page 206) ★	❑

Now that you have chosen your ingredients, you are ready to go. Let's just check:

1 Have you set your quit date? (If you are speaking to a stop-smoking advisor, that will come later.)
2 Have you decided at what time in the day you will quit?
3 Do you know what you need to do before the quit date (e.g. get your medicine)?
4 Are you mentally prepared: have you set your stop-smoking rule?

Okay. That's it. Now all you have to do is put your formula to work.

Remember to keep referring to *The SmokeFree Formula* when you need to.

Good luck!

Chapter 16

Your Questions Answered

In this chapter I will give you some specially tailored advice in response to some common questions and concerns.

Specific groups of smokers

The SmokeFree Formula is based on the idea that we are all different. So the same formula is not going to work the same for everyone. I don't know enough about you to tell you what will be your best formula, but there may be some things about you where the science can help you with your decision.

Q What if I am a teenager?

A When I was a teenager I didn't think I would live past the millennium – or particularly care. At that point I would be 44. It was too far away and, in any event, who wants to be old? I know that sounds callow and clichéd, but it is how I felt. Knowing that smoking would probably kill me was not a big worry.

At the same time, I was aware that smoking was not doing me any good and I did want to stop. People think that teenagers are not interested in stopping, but my research shows that young smokers want to stop even more than older ones and they try very often – but they find it harder.

Actually there are lots of immediate benefits to stopping when you are young. One of them is that you will simply be happier. We find in our research that most people, no matter how old they are, are happier and more satisfied with life after they stop smoking. Another benefit is the money you'll save, of course. Money is usually in pretty short supply when you are young. And then there's not smelling of cigarettes, being able to taste food better, not coughing up gunk and having a better complexion ...

I don't know, but I think that one of the reasons you find it harder to stop as a teenager is related to youth: you can always stop later on, so when the going gets tough it's just too easy to cave in. You will also probably be coming across a lot more smokers who are offering cigarettes and it is more important than in later life to feel part of the group.

In any event, what special advice can I give you to help you stop? Please bear in mind that this is just my opinion, because there is very little hard evidence to go on, but here is my advice for teenagers wanting to quit:

- Treat your quit attempt as if you were an adult smoker – doing all the things set out in this book, including making being a non-smoker part of your core identity (Ingredient 2).
- Practise ways of saying you don't smoke any more so that you don't feel under pressure when friends offer you cigarettes (see Ingredient 16).
- Use a nicotine product as a substitute if you feel any withdrawal symptoms, such as feeling irritable. And I think it would be particularly useful if you are trying to stop in the middle of exams because it will help with your concentration (see Chapter 10).

Q What if I am over 70?

A The good news about being over 70 is that statistically your chances of stopping smoking if you decide you want to are pretty good. I don't know why, but there are a few things I can think of.

One is that the benefits in terms of extending life and improving quality of life are much more immediate – particularly in terms of avoiding a heart attack and preventing escalation in the risk of cancer. Another is that when we get older, we are more selective about things we strive for, but when we do go for something we put more into it.

I also have a suspicion that the brain mechanisms underlying nicotine dependence start to weaken as our reward pathways burn out a little bit. I realise that doesn't sound very scientific, but there is some evidence that the dopamine pathway I talked about in Chapter 1 becomes less active as we get older.

So what about advice I can give to you as an older person? Generally it would be the same as anyone else except I would emphasise a few things:

- You may well already have some ill health caused by your smoking, and it's possible that it might get a little worse for a short while before it gets better. For example, for the first couple of weeks many smokers experience a worsening of their cough when trying to quit. If you have COPD this could trigger an acute event, so make sure you are ready with your inhaler and that your doctor knows what you are doing.
- If you have a problem with your kidneys (your doctor will have told you if that is the case), you should probably only take half the dose of whatever stop-smoking medicine you may be on, or just stick to nicotine products instead (see Chapter 10).
- A very common, and good, reason for quitting as an older person is to set a good example to grandchildren and to have as much time with them as possible. Your grandchildren will probably be very excited and pleased that you are stopping and that can be a great source of motivation.

Q What if I am pregnant?

A I don't need to tell you how important stopping smoking is if you are pregnant. You already know that it will make your baby's whole life better. But I also know it can be really hard and that you may feel very stressed about not being able to stop, which just makes things worse. I also know that stopping is particularly difficult if your partner smokes.

Everything I have talked about in this book applies to you when it comes to stopping, and you can use all of the ingredients except for the prescription medicines, Champix, Zyban and cytisine. (By the way, we don't know whether those medicines would harm the baby, so don't worry if you were taking one of them and then learnt you are pregnant – when pregnant women have taken them in the past we have no evidence that any damage occurred.)

So ... what else can I tell you that will help you? Here are a few things:

- Obviously it would be great if you could stop without the help of a nicotine product, but if you can't, then I would recommend using these ingredients in your formula (see Chapter 10). But I have to tell you that you are only likely to get a benefit if you use a combination of the nicotine patch and one of the faster-acting products such as the gum, lozenge or inhaler. My colleague Dr Leonie Brose recently published a study showing that it was only when pregnant smokers used a combination of this kind that they saw a benefit. I think the reason is that when you are pregnant your body gets rid of nicotine more quickly and so the dose you get from just one of the nicotine products won't be enough to stave off the urges to smoke.
- It might help to imagine what the smoke is doing to the baby inside you every time you puff on a cigarette. The toxic chemicals cross the placenta and go straight into the baby's bloodstream.
- Remember that it is never too late to stop smoking when you are pregnant. Actually most of the damage to the baby is done later in pregnancy, so please don't imagine that just because you haven't been able to stop at the beginning it isn't worth it.
- It will be incredibly tempting to go back to smoking once your baby is born. I don't have scientific evidence to guide you as to how to prevent that happening, but I think that really working on getting that non-smoker identity going could be a big help (Ingredient 2). Also, instead of thinking to yourself how great it will be once the baby is born and you can smoke again, remember that you will be exposing your baby to smoke after it's born if you carry on – and that is a very common cause of breathing problems and chest infections in babies.

Q What if I suffer from a mental health problem?

A About a quarter of all adults in Britain suffer from a diagnosed mood disorder in any one year – usually anxiety, depression or both. And of course many more experience these problems but aren't counted in these figures because they have not sought help. There are also all the other mental health problems that can afflict us – from schizophrenia to obsessive-compulsive disorder and eating disorders.

The fact is that the human brain is incredibly complex and sensitive, and there are lots of things that can go wrong with it. Often it comes from a combination of a genetic predisposition and some difficult childhood experiences, but sometimes it just comes out of the blue for no obvious reason.

You might be worried that whatever problems you are suffering from will be made worse by stopping – but that won't happen. In fact it is usually quite the opposite. The only thing is that stopping is a bit more difficult if you are currently suffering from a mental health problem.

I'm sorry to say that a lot of mental-health professionals are not very well clued-up on smoking, and I've heard reports of them trying to put smokers off quitting, saying things like, 'You've got quite enough on your plate without adding this to your stresses,' or 'Smoking is probably helping manage your symptoms, so it's best not to stop at the moment.' (In fact quite a lot of mental health professionals smoke themselves, so may not be as engaged with your desire to stop as you would like!)

Here are some things to remember that should help:

- There is no reason why you can't use Champix or one of the nicotine products (Ingredients 12, 10 and 11). Champix has been specifically shown to help smokers with schizophrenia and depression to stop. Some doctors will say you can't use Champix if you have a mental health problem, but please tell them: that's not what the evidence or the guidance from the medicine regulators tells us.

- Using some form of psychological support for your mental health problem can help with stopping smoking. I know it's hard to get to see a qualified psychologist who can give you CBT (cognitive behavioural therapy), so if you can't get to see someone, you could try one of the Internet-based courses. (If you just put 'Online CBT' into Google you will see a lot of sites. Ones worth considering are Beating the Blues (<http://www.beatingtheblues.co.uk>), Living Life to the Full (<http://www.llttf.com>) and MoodGYM (<http://www.moodgym.anu.edu.au>).
- If you are taking a medicine for schizophrenia, your doctor will need to review your dose and you will probably be able to reduce it as time goes by. That is because once you stop smoking your body does not get rid of your medicine so quickly, so it can be effective at a lower dose. If your doctor doesn't know about this, ask him or her to look it up!
- Don't get confused by the nicotine-withdrawal symptoms into thinking that your mental-health symptoms have got worse. Irritability, sleep problems and many other reactions are normal when you stop smoking and go away quite quickly. You might even feel spaced out or floaty. If you are using a nicotine product, you can take more of it to reduce these symptoms.
- You might need to take Champix or your nicotine product for longer than the usual 8 to 12 weeks. Your doctor should be willing and able to give you a prescription for as much as you need and for as long as you need it.

Q What if I already have an illness caused by smoking?

A You obviously have an immediate reason for trying to quit, and the benefits of stopping will probably show themselves quite soon. For example, if you suffer from lung problems, I expect your breathing to improve a bit and for you to be less likely to experience acute attacks that mean you have to go to hospital. If you have had a heart attack, then the research shows that you are much less likely to have another one if you stop smoking. Even if you have lung cancer, your chances of getting better are increased by stopping smoking.

My best piece of advice if your health is already being affected by your smoking, is to find a good stop-smoking advisor (Ingredient 4) and work with them and The SmokeFree Formula to help you get off cigarettes.

Q What if I use illicit drugs?

A Our research tells us that smokers who also use illicit drugs, even cannabis, are less successful when it comes to freeing themselves from their cigarette habit.

I can't tell you about any really good studies that tell us what is going to work best for you, but I would give serious thought to whether it might be best to kick the whole lot in one go. I have two friends who did that and the transformation in them was incredibly positive. They really took being fit and healthy into their identity and haven't looked back.

The other thing I would suggest, if it is proving difficult to get off nicotine completely, is to continue to use a nicotine product for as long as is necessary (see Chapter 10). Don't think you have to go cold turkey – these products really do help. Don't worry about using as much as you like for as long as you like – and try out different products, probably using two or more at a time.

Q What if I have an alcohol problem?

A Almost a quarter of smokers have an alcohol problem compared with less than ten per cent of the general adult population. Actually far more of us drink too much alcohol, but not so much as to badly affect our life at the moment, and we do not *need* to drink.

Having had an alcohol problem in the past does not affect your chances of stopping smoking, but having one at the moment does reduce your chances a bit.

A lot of people who work in the field of alcohol dependence believe that stopping smoking will make your chances of recovering from alcohol dependence worse, but the evidence on that is very clear: it certainly does not harm your chances, and it may improve them. So you shouldn't worry at all about the idea of stopping smoking.

There's not much more I can tell you, apart from to say that, because you will probably find it more difficult, you should seriously consider using two or more nicotine products (see Chapter 10) for as long as you need to.

Q What if I do not smoke every day?

A There is no safe level of smoking, so you are right to want to stop. The main risk from light smoking is heart disease.

Most people can't understand how someone who doesn't smoke every day can possibly find it hard to stop smoking. But I know that it is difficult because my research tells me that even very light smokers struggle not to smoke when they find themselves in situations where they are used to having a cigarette. You might remember in Chapter 1 that I told you how nicotine from cigarettes gives you the urge to smoke in situations when you'd normally light up.

So what can I tell you about how best to stop? Well, not much from the scientific evidence, because very light smokers tend to get excluded from our studies. But I'll tell you what I think:

- Like any other smoker, you will have to work on transforming your identity so that smoking is not part of it (Ingredient 2). You are not the kind of person who smokes at parties, when out with friends or in any situation.
- For the time being, I would recommend using one of the faster-acting nicotine products (such as gum, lozenge or spray) to use, instead of smoking, if you really feel a strong urge to smoke (see Chapter 10).
- You will also have to work on your response when your friends offer you a cigarette or ask if you are coming outside for a smoke (see Ingredient 16). What will you tell them?

Q What if I am overweight?

A It sometimes seems a miracle that we are not all overweight. If you give your dog or cat as much food as it wants, whenever it wants, it will get fat. We evolved to take advantage of food when it is there, and it requires self-control for most of us not to eat delicious food if it is available, even when we are not hungry.

A lot of smokers are overweight – just like the rest of the population. If that applies to you, the possibility that you will put on more weight when you stop smoking is no doubt something very much on your mind.

I already told you about exercise and health snacks as ways of limiting the weight gain while also dealing with the urges to smoke. I would strongly advise you to use those ingredients in your SmokeFree Formula.

Really set about making and following a clear, structured plan for what you are going to do – particularly when it comes to exercise. If you don't already do it, please give serious thought to planning 30 minutes of brisk walking into your day. I realise that this is not always easy, particularly if you don't have nice places to walk nearby. But if you do have somewhere with a bit of greenery within half a mile – take advantage of it.

If you work within 30 minutes walk from home, then walk instead of taking the bus or driving. Something that can be very easy is to take the stairs instead of lifts and always walk up escalators instead of just standing on them. Every little really does help.

Everyone has different tactics for keeping a healthy weight. As I mentioned before, personally, I weigh myself every day on digital scales. If I am above my limit I eat less until I am below it again. It doesn't matter why I am above – it is a hard-and-fast rule.

Or, if that sounds too much to cope with, you can just accept that you will put on some weight and deal with it later. Frankly, smoking is the bigger threat to your health right now.

Put simply: you have two options. Either you are going to do something to keep your weight down or you are going to gain weight.

The thing is to make sure that you choose which option to go for rather than leaving it to chance.

Whatever you weigh now, one thing you can be sure of is this: even if you put on more weight while quitting, you will still be much healthier than when you were smoking.

Frequently asked questions

This next section lists some of the most common questions I hear and tells you where in the book to find answers to help you.

The SmokeFree Formula will help you answer these and other questions based on the latest scientific evidence. The answers to these questions will be the ingredients in a stop-smoking formula that you will create each time you try to stop.

Q If I feel ready to stop now, should I delay to give me time to prepare?

A I wouldn't advise this unless you are going to seek help. You should strike while the iron is hot, and you can always seek help or a stop-smoking product if you start to struggle. See Chapter 5 and Ingredient 1.

Q Should I seek help from a specialist counsellor?

A Yes, if there is a good one available – this can more than treble your chance of stopping forever. See Ingredient 4.

Q Should I phone a telephone helpline?

A If there is a good service available this is a good option as it can improve your chances of stopping permanently. See Ingredient 5.

Q Should I use hypnotherapy?

A In my opinion this is probably not worth paying for but if it is something that attracts you and you know all the facts I wouldn't want to put you off. It may be better than nothing but it does not have as much evidence to support it as the (free) specialist support provided by the NHS. See Ingredient 4.

Q Are there any good stop-smoking websites?

A Websites can definitely help. StopAdvisor has the most extensive evidence behind it of all the free ones available to you. See Ingredient 7.

Q Are there any good stop-smoking smartphone apps?

A Apps can almost certainly help. One called SF28 has been tested and has the most extensive evidence behind it at the moment. See Ingredient 9.

Q Should I cut down gradually or abruptly?

A It is best to stop abruptly if you possibly can – this tends to give better results. See Ingredient 1.

Q When is the best time of day to smoke my last cigarette?

A As far as we can tell, it is really up to your personal preference. See Chapter 5 for more on ways to quit.

Q What can I do instead of smoking when I get stressed?

A There are lots of things you can do: simple relaxation exercises can help and so can breathing exercises and some form of physical activity. See Chapter 14.

Q Should I tell people I'm stopping or keep it quiet?

A It doesn't seem to make any difference to your success, so it's entirely your preference. See Ingredient 16.

Q Should I use a nicotine product?

A It can help, but you must make sure you use it properly – make sure you use enough and use it for long enough. See Chapter 10.

Q How long should I use my nicotine product for?

A You should use your product for at least six weeks, and then as long as you feel you need it.

Q Should I use one of the prescription medicines now available?

A Yes, they can help if you use them properly. Varenicline (Champix) is generally more effective than bupropion (Zyban). See Chapter 11.

Q Should I get rid of my cigarettes and ashtrays?

A I think so. There will be times when you will be tempted, and anything you can do to allow that moment to pass without smoking could make all the difference. See Ingredient 23.

Q Should I stay away from bars and/or alcohol?

A It is probably best to do this for a while. Alcohol has messed up so many quit attempts. If you do go for a drink, I strongly recommend that you plan in advance how you are going to deal with the temptation to smoke. See Ingredient 21.

Q Should I try to get more exercise?

A Yes, I think this is worth doing. We know that exercise reduces cigarette cravings and makes you feel better. The key thing is to find a form that suits you – it doesn't have to be strenuous. See   Ingredient 24.

Q Should I diet to try to avoid putting on weight?

A Probably not, but I would carry a healthy snack around with you. See Ingredient 29.

Q What is the best way of combating cravings?

A There are a number of things you can do: taking stop-smoking medicines, taking nicotine products, chewing glucose tablets, doing small amounts of exercise and doing breathing exercises. See chapters 10, 11, and 14.

Q Should I try to find someone to stop with?

A If you can do it easily, this might help. I suggest you plan how you are going to support each other – e.g. with texts or phone calls every day. See Ingredient 18.

Q Should I switch to electronic cigarettes?

A These can help you stop smoking. The various electronic cigarettes are very different, and some give little or no nicotine, so be prepared to do some homework and try different ones until you find one that suits you. See Ingredient 11.

Q Is there any benefit from just cutting down?

A The main benefit is that you will be more likely to go on to stop later, even if you don't intend to now. You will get the most benefit if you use a nicotine product to fill the gaps because that will stop you puffing harder on your remaining cigarettes and undoing all the benefits of smoking fewer of them. See Chapter 10.

Chapter 17

If you Slip Up

One of the great pleasures of my job is bumping into people who have stopped smoking during one of my studies. They look healthy and are happy in their lives as non-smokers. But sometimes the picture is not so rosy. Sometimes they have gone back to smoking. Sheila was one such person. She worked on the till in a hospital canteen and had stopped smoking as part of a study I did.

Sheila had not smoked – not a single cigarette – for three months. I remembered her: a kind, gentle woman with a young family. When I saw her I asked how things were going. I fully expected she would tell me everything was fine. When she said she had gone back to smoking, I was taken aback – and felt a pang of sadness. What had happened?

She said nothing much – she hadn't been craving a cigarette. Her life was fine – no great stresses. But she had been out with friends one evening. Probably about a third of her friends smoked. It was before the days of smoking bans and she was sitting in the pub and one of her friends lit up. She offered a cigarette around – not to Sheila because she did not smoke any more. But something clicked in Sheila's brain and she thought 'why not?'

Our studies confirm what many people already believe: most smokers who go back to smoking do not intend to. What they intend is to smoke one or two cigarettes – maybe a packet – and then carry on as ex-smokers. Of course, in 90 per cent of cases that is not what happens. One cigarette leads to another, and within days or weeks they are smoking regularly again. There are different ways of tackling these slips, and there is some evidence to draw on to help smokers to choose how they want to move on from a mistake.

These are last-resort tactics. If you're thinking: 'It might be okay to have one because these methods will help me get back on track' – *please don't.*

The evidence shows that if you have one cigarette you're much more likely to go back permanently. I'm going to tell you a couple of things to give you a better chance if you do make a mistake. But, as always, the best way is not to have a single puff.

Intensify

If you smoke a cigarette or two, it tells you something important: whatever you are doing to resist the desire to smoke is not enough. The logical thing to do then, is to do more of it. If you are using a nicotine product, you should increase the dose. Whatever ingredients you are using, go through them and see whether you can up your game with it – are you really doing it properly? Most important of all, I think, you need to recommit to being completely smoke-free.

It is very unusual to actively decide to go back to smoking after the first slip. What usually happens is that you put your quit attempt on hold while you have a cigarette or two, or perhaps even a packet. But you have every intention of going back to the quit attempt afterwards.

But that is easier said than done. If you are going to get back on track, you will need to have a very good look at what led you to have the cigarette and what you can do to prevent it happening again.

It may be that the cravings got to you. In that case, if you are using a nicotine product it would be a very good idea to increase the amount you use. Everyone is different and you may simply not be using enough to keep the cravings at bay. If you are not already using a patch plus a faster acting product, then I strongly recommend you do that.

I would also recommend that you go through the ingredients you have signed up to, and look at whether you need to modify any of them. For example, if you slipped up because you were out with smoking friends, perhaps you should review whether you should avoid these kinds of situations in future.

The most important thing is that, if you are going to carry on with this quit attempt, *you must recommit to total abstinence, starting now.*

Rosalind – 50 years old – *stopped abruptly*

An ex-smoker who does not regret having smoked but knows she will never smoke again.

I took up smoking aged 16. Initially ten cigarettes would last a week. By the time I was 19, I was smoking 30 a day, including in the middle of the night if I woke up. Part of this may have been because I was in a relationship with a very heavy smoker. Smoking was something we did together. I enjoyed smoking and prioritised it over other things – e.g. if I was short of money.

We now know that quite a lot of smokers will buy cigarettes rather than food if they are short of money – yet another sign as to how addictive smoking can be.

Giving up the first time, when I was 31, was very easy. I was pregnant and could not bear the thought of damaging my baby. I do not remember having any urges to smoke. I also gave up alcohol, tea and coffee as I suddenly couldn't stand the taste of them, nor could I smell food cooking without feeling nauseous. This lasted for the entire pregnancy.

I hear quite often about women going off smoking during pregnancy – just as they suddenly go off some foods. We don't know what causes this, but how wonderful it would be if we could bottle it!

Some time after my son was born, when I went back to work, I started smoking again. I didn't smoke as

Two thirds of women who stop during pregnancy go back to smoking within the first year afterwards.

much as before since my husband was disapproving, but I smoked regularly at work and socially but never in the home. I don't remember having particular urges to smoke at home.

The second quit was with my second pregnancy, and was a similar experience to the first one. I abstained from smoking for a longer time after my daughter was born. After a time, both my husband and I smoked occasionally – he seemed able to do this without reverting to a regular smoker but I gradually became a daily smoker – at work and when I was out but never at home.

Gradual resumption of smoking is common after a quit attempt. Sometimes it can be months before smokers go back to their previous level of smoking.

One day I came home to find some old friends visiting and became aware of the smell of smoke on my clothes. I was ashamed. I 'quit' within a week or so of that experience. However I did lapse a few times. The last time was when I had severe and persistent back pain. I bought some cigarettes to smoke at a corporate event (attended with my husband, who still smoked at this type of event – to 'fit in' with his customers, he thought). I smoked almost all the packet of ten. On the way home I had to stop the car to be ill. The combination of pain and nausea was dreadful.

If your mind set is right, even a lapse like this one is not the end of the quit attempt.

That was my last smoking experience – approximately 17 years ago. My husband also stopped smoking completely within a year or two of that.

Rosalind stopping was very likely responsible for her husband stopping – two for the price of one!

I still dream of being a smoker quite frequently and it's always in a pleasant dream. Awake, I cannot conceive of any situation when I would smoke. I have enormous empathy with smokers and appreciate the pleasure that smoking gives. However, it's not a pleasure worth the health risks for me and hasn't been for a very long time.

Rosalind has not become an ardent anti-smoker and recognises that it can give pleasure – but she has clearly moved on to a new phase in her life in which cigarettes do not have a place.

Change tack

It might be that the ingredients you have chosen are not quite right for this quit attempt. You will probably have quite a good idea which ones these are. It could be that they proved difficult to use properly or perhaps you were doing it right but it didn't work for you this time. If so, then you can go back to the ingredient list and see what else you can do.

I have a colleague and friend, Dr Eva Králíková, who runs a stop-smoking clinic in Prague and she gets very high success rates. She provides very good behavioural support and a choice of stop-smoking medicines, which I'm sure contribute to this. One thing she does which might also make a difference is to say to her smokers that if one thing isn't working, they can try something else. So if they are using a nicotine product and not getting on very well with it, they can switch to varenicline or vice versa. This seems logical for those clients who still feel they have enough mental energy to keep going with the quit attempt. It's not for everyone, but it may help some people and this is something you could consider.

So if you lapse, think about going through all your ingredients and seeing if it would make sense to add some or change some. The worst that can happen is that you go back to smoking anyway. But it could get you back on the right path.

Take a break

Sometimes the best thing you can do is to relax, go back to smoking and build up your reserves to have another go later. The most important thing is not to feel bad, but just to think about what happened and use that information to plan better the next time you try to stop.

Stopping smoking can take its toll on your mental reserves. Any kind of self-control does. If you have children, you may have noticed that when they have had to behave themselves for the day – perhaps when with their grandparents – the moment they get in the car to go home they often start to act up. Their human brain has got tired of keeping the animal brain under control. Now it's tired and can't keep up the act any more …

It's not very different with stopping smoking. If you slip up, it's important to remember that you can recover. But if you really don't think you can carry on, that's okay. You can feel pleased with what you have achieved, and you should know that it is only positive.

So, let's say you have decided that you can't carry on with this quit attempt. The next question is: how long should you leave it before having another go? My research tells me that it's best to wait until you are ready – not to force yourself to try again too soon. It may be weeks, months or even perhaps a year for some people. You will know when you are truly ready again.

In the meantime, my research tells me that you will probably be smoking less than you were – at least in terms of number of cigarettes per day, and that is no bad thing.

If you were using a nicotine product in your quit attempt, I think that it would make sense to carry on using it to help you keep your smoking levels down. We know that using nicotine products to help you cut down is a good predictor of successfully stopping in the future.

Tomorrow is another day

If you have gone back to smoking, it will have followed one of these scenarios:

You never got properly started

Sometimes when you get to the quit point, you turn the key on the ignition for your quit attempt … and nothing happens. The battery is flat and something inside you says: 'This is not the right time'. So you carry on smoking.

This can happen if you have left it rather too long between deciding to quit and the quit date itself. Or if you are just not mentally prepared for quitting. Or something has happened in your life that takes priority.

Sometimes the starter motor turns over but your quit attempt never ignites. You last for a few hours, and then the battery dies and you have a cigarette. Again, the force behind the quit attempt wasn't there. This can happen if you haven't psyched yourself up enough. Or if you've psyched yourself up too much! It can also happen if you have spent a lot of your mental energy in trying to cut down before you finally quit.

Whatever the reason, about a quarter of attempts to stop smoking don't get past the first day, so the main thing is not to beat yourself up about it. Just note it and learn from the experience.

You will probably immediately be thinking about stopping again. My advice is to leave it a while – don't force it. You will know when the time is right to give it another go. Look for the opportunity, and when it comes, take it.

In the meantime, you can certainly be thinking about the ingredients you used this time, and whether you might want to change them next time. For example, if you decided not to tell people you were quitting this time, you might want to try that next time to give yourself a bit more of a kick-start.

If you are using a nicotine product, then you might want to carry on using it and even increase the amount to stop your smoking going back up to previous levels. In effect, you will have turned your quit attempt into a 'cut-down attempt'.

On page 145, I told you about cutting down when you have no immediate plans to stop. The key message was that if you do this with the aid of a nicotine product there is good evidence that it will speed your path ultimately to stopping – even when that is not your intention right now.

It was too much of an uphill struggle

You've lasted a day, or perhaps a few weeks, trying your very best to avoid smoking but it's all getting too much. The cravings are too strong, your mood takes a nose-dive, your morale is sapped and you cave in.

You probably didn't think you were going back to smoking – you probably decided just to smoke a few cigarettes, maybe a packet and then you would get back on the wagon, but that is not how it turned out.

The first thing to do when this happens is relax. It's okay. You didn't lose anything. You probably saved some money, gained some health and created an experience you could learn from.

Talking of which – when you feel you have the energy and motivation, go back to your list of ingredients and do two things to prepare for next time:

1 Decide if you want to choose different ingredients.
2 Think about how you could use the ingredients better.

For example, let's say you decided not to use any nicotine products or a stop-smoking medicine. If you went back to smoking because the cravings were so strong you couldn't resist them, or you were getting so grumpy you became unbearable to live with, perhaps that tells you that next time it would be worth giving one of these ingredients a try.

Or, if you decided to use a nicotine product and still the cravings got to you, you need to think about whether you used enough of it and whether you would be better adding a second product (remember that a patch plus a faster-acting product typically gives the best results).

Or if you were using one of the faster-acting nicotine products and got caught out by a craving, you should look at how you were using it. Were you waiting until you got the craving before starting to chew the gum or suck the lozenge, etc.? Remember that it can take up to 30 minutes for these products to give you enough nicotine, so you should be using them regularly throughout the day and, if you know you are going to be in a situation where you will be tempted, you should start using your product before you get there.

Or perhaps you decided you were going to try to change your

routine to avoid the smoking triggers, but when it came to it, you never got a good plan going for doing that. Now you may have ideas for better ways of doing that.

Basically, you want to learn as much from the experience as possible so that next time (and there definitely will be a next time), you can create a better formula.

Something happened!

When interviewing ex-smokers I asked them whether they had tried to stop before the successful quit attempt and what led them back to smoking. A very common theme is: something happened!

They were doing fine. Sure they were tempted every now and then, but they were perfectly happy not smoking, and then – BANG! – out of the blue they got hit by something that made them reach for a cigarette.

Mostly it is something bad – they lose a job, a close relative dies, they break up with a partner, they have a traffic accident … Then in a moment, months or years of being a non-smoker went out of the window and they either smoked a cigarette they got from someone else or very often they went out and bought a packet themselves.

If this is what happened to you, rest assured you are not alone.

The big question is, what happens next, and how can you learn from this to make sure it doesn't happen the next time? The chances are that you got a lot of your formula right, so I would not be thinking of making big changes to it. Keep most of your ingredients and just focus on the ones that didn't quite do the job.

If you had managed the cravings well with a stop-smoking medicine or nicotine product, if you had found a really good stop-smoking advisor and if you had an app that particularly worked for you, there is no need to change unless you are looking for novelty.

What you may not have quite got right was your mental approach. If you had really become a non-smoker in the core of your being, you would no more have thought about reaching for a cigarette in response to the 'something' as you would sticking your head in a bucket of water – why would you do that? In that case, you might want to pay special attention to your thought processes the next time you try to stop. You could start thinking about whether the cigarettes you smoked made the situation better or even made you *feel* better about the situation. From the ex-smokers I talk to, my guess is that they didn't.

Another thing to consider is whether you had got over the cravings as fully as you thought you had. On reflection, you might have had a few near misses in the lead up to the 'something'. If so, perhaps you stopped using your medicine or nicotine product a little too soon. We are all different and it would be ridiculous to imagine that everyone needs to use the products for exactly the same amount of time.

If you were still having twinges of cravings, next time you might want to keep a nicotine product on you at all times for the first few weeks. You can make a very clear plan that if anything happens to make you want to smoke – you will use that product instead. That is a promise you make to yourself. After that, you can see how you feel – but for the first few weeks you will get your nicotine from something other than a cigarette.

Those are just a couple of examples. If we were sitting together having a post-mortem on your quit attempt we could discuss each of the ingredients more fully. But hopefully I've given you some ideas to think about. This time your formula was pretty close – next time it could be just right.

You were in a group of smokers ...

This path back to smoking seems so unnecessary and yet it is so common. If you have a lot of smoking friends or your partner smokes, it is harder to stop. You already knew that. So you chose ingredients to deal with it.

The chances are you were caught by surprise. You hadn't quite got your new identity worked out as 'someone who doesn't smoke even when friends are lighting up all around them'. This identity is not neutral: it's a very positive and definite statement about who you are. It needs to be someone you feel comfortable being – someone you want to be more than 'someone who smokes with their friends'.

That kind of non-smoker could be someone who:

- Uses a nicotine product such as an electronic cigarette instead.
- Stays inside with the non-smokers while the smokers go outside for a smoke.

- Goes outside and chats with smoking friends but is not tempted to smoke.
- Uses the opportunity when others are smoking to go off and do something else.
- Makes friendly fun of smokers who have to go outside to smoke.
- Or something else that works for you.

I am assuming here that everything else in your quit attempt was going okay. If your cravings weren't under control, then there will be other ingredients to look at changing or using differently. But if everything was fine, apart from the fact that you fell in with your smoking friends, then you know exactly what you have to work on next time.

You'd had a few drinks

This often goes hand in hand with the smoking-friends thing. There's no getting away from it. The next time you stop, you're going to have to get your ingredients working to tackle this one.

Remember that alcohol loosens your inhibitions, undermines your self-control, puts you in a frame of mind when you don't think about the future (not even the next morning, let alone the next 20 years!), and it makes you think about smoking …

I don't know whether this will work, but it can't hurt: *before* your next quit attempt, see if you can loosen the association between drinking and smoking by deliberately not smoking when you are drinking. So you can smoke your head off at other times but when you have alcohol in your system you can't smoke. You can use one of the nicotine products instead if you like – but *you can't smoke*. If you can achieve this for a while (at least some of the time), when you next come to stop, the theory is it may be less of a problem for you.

But that is all speculation. The main thing is to use your experience this time to guide how you deal with alcohol next time. Perhaps it would be best to avoid drinking for a while. And, while you are at it, review the other ingredients just to check what was working and what might need some tweaking.

Whatever the reason

You may have gone back to smoking for some other reason. Perhaps you put on too much weight, got too difficult to live with, missed being a smoker, felt something was missing from your life, forgot you were supposed to have stopped …

Whatever the reason you went back to smoking, the things to remember are:

1 Don't worry. Relax. You did well.
2 Don't feel you have to have another go right away; leave time for your batteries to recharge. You will know when the time is right to try again.
3 Seriously consider substituting another nicotine product for some of your cigarettes right now.
4 Keep *The SmokeFree Formula* somewhere reasonably handy and dip into it every now and then for ideas about what you are going to do next time.
5 Keep your eyes and ears open for other people around you who are stopping and see how they are getting along.
6 When the time comes to try again – it might be after a few months or it might be as long as a year (I wouldn't leave it much longer than that) – dust off this book and use your experience from this and past quit attempts to make a new, better, formula.
7 Remember: *the next time could be the last time you will ever have to try.*

Conclusion

I've told you everything that I think science can teach you about how to give yourself the best possible chance of quitting. Now you can put that knowledge into action. Remember: every cigarette you don't smoke is a success. Every cigarette you don't smoke is a step to a happier, healthier life. Every cigarette you don't smoke brings you closer to the day when you have no desire to smoke – there are no cravings to resist; you just don't smoke.

I've seen a lot of people who were scared about quitting, who didn't think they were going to make it. People, perhaps, like you. But they did. They set themselves a clear rule – no more cigarettes – and they stuck to it. If they slipped up, they didn't give up the fight, they counted it as a step along the road to permanent success. Their persistence paid off. There are literally millions of people, many of them just like you, who are now living lives free from the hold that smoking had on them.

I've given you my help. But the achievement, and the fruits of success – they're all yours.

Appendix 1: Things that I Don't Think Will Help

I'll now tell you something about products, services and ideas that didn't make it into my list of ingredients because I don't think they will help, or at least not as much as something else that you could easily get for free.

If there is something in this list that particularly grabs you and you really want to give it a go, fine. But when it comes to parting with your cash, please don't be taken in by claims of success or testimonials – as I said on page 121, they really don't mean anything.

If you want to be an informed consumer of one of these therapies, then here are some questions you can ask the person promoting them before signing up:

1 How many people received this therapy in the last year?
2 Do you routinely follow them up after, say, four weeks or more to ask them whether they are still not smoking?
3 How many said they had not smoked at all since they started your therapy – even if they never finished it?
4 Of every person who *started* your therapy in the last year how many succeeded for at least four weeks?

If the answer to any of these is 'I don't know' or 'I'm not telling you', then I advise you to walk away! If they can answer these questions and claim a success rate of more than 60 per cent, be very wary.

Obviously you are in no position to check that they are telling the truth and there is nothing to stop them making the numbers up.

To give you something to compare with: the best stop-smoking services – which use a combination of behavioural support and one of the stop-smoking medicines – will give a four-week quit rate of about 50 per cent. Every single one of the quits will be confirmed by having the smoker come back and blow into a carbon monoxide monitor. Everyone who sets a quit date and does not come back for that four-week test will be counted as a smoker.

So here are things that have never been properly evaluated or have been tested and found not to help you stop.

Acupuncture

Acupuncture involves inserting small needles into the skin in particular spots in order to achieve some medical outcome. There's quite good evidence it can help with pain relief. But it has been studied as a way of helping smokers to stop and no benefit was found.

There is a variant called 'electro-acupuncture' that has some fairly big claims made for its ability to cure addiction. With this, the needles have a small electric current put through them. This doesn't have any good evidence to support it either.

Anti-anxiety drugs

You might think that tranquilisers, or any drug that helped control your anxiety, might help you stop smoking. But they have been tested in clinical trials and didn't help. I think the reason for this is that – although stress is often given as a reason for smoking – that is not the same thing as anxiety. And pills that reduce general anxiety levels do not necessarily stop you feeling the kind of stress that makes you reach for a cigarette.

Aromatherapy

This usually involves a combination of fragrant oils and relaxation, often with music in the background. It has never been properly tested as a way to help you stop, and there's no reason to think it would work.

Laser therapy

There are various forms of this, but it usually involves shining a low-power laser beam at some part of your body – such as in your ear. There is no reason to imagine that this would help.

Lobeline

Lobeline is a chemical that looks rather like nicotine, and scientists hoped that it would reduce the nicotine cravings. Sadly, when they came to try it out – it didn't.

Naltrexone

Naltrexone is a drug that blocks the opioid receptors in your brain. It is very effective in reversing the effects of heroin or morphine if you overdose on these drugs. Some people think that part of nicotine's rewarding properties are due to it mimicking drugs such as heroin. This has led to studies which looked at whether naltrexone would help smokers to stop. So far no one has been able to find a convincing effect.

Nicotine vaccines

You may have read about these. Millions of pounds, dollars and euros have been (and continue to be) spent developing them. The reason is that if a really good vaccine can be discovered, it could make smoking history!

The theory behind a vaccine is that it would stimulate your body to produce 'antibodies' to nicotine, just as flu jabs and other inoculations do to germs that enter your bloodstream. These antibodies would attach themselves to the nicotine molecules and stop them entering your brain. If your body can be persuaded to produce enough of these for long enough, it would not matter how much you smoked, no nicotine would enter your brain. In effect you would be immune to any effects of nicotine. Since it is nicotine that your brain is seeking, you would simply go off smoking.

Alas, we are nowhere near that. The technical challenge of making a vaccine that does this well is proving too great. That is not to say that we could never see an effective vaccine, just that right now things are not looking very promising. So don't pin your hopes on it.

Psychoanalysis

Psychoanalysis comes in many different forms. Freud and Jung are probably the best-known originators of this approach to improving mental health. The general idea is that your unconscious mind has unresolved issues that are causing you emotional and behavioural problems, and if they are brought to conscious awareness, they can be addressed to the benefit of your mental health.

How far this form of therapy helps with other psychological problems is hotly debated, but there isn't good evidence that it helps with stopping smoking. And I can't see how it would. I don't think the unconscious processes involved in smoking are repressed sexual urges or even a death wish – at least not for most smokers. It's nicotine.

Silver acetate chewing gum

You don't see this much nowadays. When you chew this gum it makes cigarettes taste disgusting, so it is a form of 'aversion' therapy. This has been tested and not found to be effective.

I think a big problem with it is that if you want to avoid the unpleasant taste you just have to stop chewing the gum!

Appendix 2: The Benefits of Quitting Smoking

Here is a ready reference guide on the benefits of quitting smoking. All of these are based on the latest scientific evidence. I thought it would be worthwhile just to list them so that you know.

The most important causes of death from smoking are marked in **bold**.

If it's not on the list, it's not something for which we have good evidence to call a benefit. For example, a lot of doctors and some websites say that stopping smoking reduces blood pressure, but it doesn't.

Smoking is linked to all of these, and when you stop, your risk is reduced compared with continuing to smoke:

- Aortic aneurism (causing rupture of the main blood supply from the heart)
- Back pain
- Buerger's disease (leading to amputations)
- Cancer of the bladder
- Cancer of the cervix
- **Cancer of the lung, trachea and bronchus**
- Cancer of the mouth
- Cancer of the oesophagus
- Cancer of the pancreas

- Cancer of the stomach
- **Chronic obstructive pulmonary disease (COPD) (Bronchitis and emphysema)**
- Death of baby during childbirth
- Dementia
- Diabetes
- Early menopause (stopping periods)
- Fetal growth stunting (delaying development of the baby in the womb)
- Gum disease (leading to tooth loss)
- **Heart disease (leading to angina, heart attack and heart failure)**
- Impotence (inability to get an erection)
- Infertility
- Leukaemia (cancer of the blood cells)
- Miscarriage
- Mood disturbance
- Osteoporosis (leading to broken bones)
- Peripheral vascular disease (leading to amputation)
- Pneumonia
- Skin wrinkles
- Stroke
- Ulcer of the stomach and duodenum

Smoking makes the following diseases worse:

- Asthma
- Crohn's disease (inflamed bowel)
- Graves' disease (overactive thyroid gland)
- Multiple Sclerosis